Django Full Stack Development with Python

Stop Dreaming, Start Building. Conquer Front-End, Back-End, and Everything In-Between and more!

Katie Millie

Django Full Stack Development with Python

Stop Dreaming, Start Building. Conquer Front-End, Back-End, and Everything In-Between and more!

By

Katie Millie

Copyright notice

Copyright © 2024 Katie Millie. All Rights Reserved.

The entirety of the content found on this website, spanning from textual elements to visual assets such as images, graphics, logos, and audiovisual materials, is safeguarded by copyright legislation. No part of this content may be replicated, disseminated, transmitted, exhibited, or employed in any manner without the explicit written authorization from Katie Millie.

Any unauthorized duplication, reproduction, or distribution of the materials featured on this website is strictly forbidden and could lead to legal consequences.

Your compliance with the intellectual property rights of Katie Millie is deeply appreciated.

Table of Contents

INTRODUCTION
Chapter 1
    Why Web Development Matters
        Unveiling the Full-Stack Developer: A Journey into Django Full Stack Development with Python
            A Glimpse into the Django & Python Powerhouse: Unleashing the Potential of Full-Stack Development
Chapter 2
    Setting Up Your Python Development Environment for Django Full Stack Development
        Demystifying Variables, Data Types, and Operators in Python
            Mastering Control Flow with Conditional Statements and Loops in Python
                Building Reusable Code with Functions in Django Full Stack Development
Chapter 3
    Understanding the MVC Architecture in Django Full Stack Development
        Installing and Configuring Django for Full Stack Development
            Creating Your First Django Project: Let's Get Coding!
Chapter 4
    The Backbone: Models and Object-Relational Mapping (ORM)
        Interacting with Databases Using Django's ORM

Performing CRUD Operations (Create, Read, Update, Delete) with Ease

Chapter 5
- Understanding URL Patterns and Mapping
- Crafting Views: The Heart of User Interaction
- Handling User Input and Form Processing

Chapter 6
- Introduction to Django Templates (Jinja2)
- Using Variables, Filters, and Tags to Dynamically Generate Content
- Creating Beautiful and Functional User Interfaces

Chapter 7
- Unveiling the Front-End: HTML, CSS, and JavaScript
- Styling Websites with CSS: Defining Visual Appeal
- Adding Interactivity with JavaScript: Making Websites Dynamic
- Integrating Front-End Technologies with Django Templates

Chapter 8
- Implementing User Registration, Login, and Logout Functionality
- Managing User Permissions and Access Control
- Securing Your Django Application

Chapter 9
- Managing Images, CSS, JavaScript, and Other Static Content
- Uploading and Handling User-Generated

- Content (Media)
  - Optimizing Static Files for Performance

Chapter 10
- Django Admin Panel: Effortless Content Management
  - Managing Models and Data Efficiently with the Admin Panel
    - Extending the Admin Functionality for Custom Needs

Chapter 11
- Choosing the Right Hosting Platform for Your Django Application
  - Configuring Your Application for Production Deployment
    - Setting Up Continuous Integration and Continuous Delivery (CI/CD)

Chapter 12
- Beyond the Basics: Exploring Advanced Django Features
  - Django Forms: Creating Robust Forms for User Input
    - Django Signals and Middleware: Customizing Django Behavior

Chapter 13
- Building Your Developer Portfolio: Putting Your Skills to the Test
  - Implementing Advanced Features and User Experience Enhancements
    - Showcasing Your Skills and Landing Your Dream Job

Conclusion

Appendix
- Common Python Libraries and Tools for Web Development
  - Troubleshooting Tips and Error Handling in Django
    - Glossary of terms

INTRODUCTION

Unleash Your Inner Web Architect: Django Full Stack Development with Python

Have you ever dreamt of crafting dynamic web applications that come alive with a click? Do you crave the power to build not just websites, but sophisticated online experiences that captivate users and solve real-world problems? Then step into the electrifying world of Django Full Stack Development with Python, your gateway to becoming a web development rockstar!

This book is not your average, dry programming manual. It's a hands-on adventure, a thrilling quest that equips you with the knowledge and tools to conquer the digital frontier. Forget complex jargon and intimidating code – here, we break down Django, the Python web framework giant, into bite-sized, easy-to-understand chunks.

Why Django? Why Python?

The answer is simple: power, elegance, and efficiency. Python, a programming language lauded for its readability,becomes your magic wand. It's clear syntax feels almost like writing plain English, allowing you to focus on the creative spark, not wrestling with code. Django, built on top of Python, is your architectural masterpiece in waiting. It provides a robust foundation with pre-built tools and functionalities – like a preassembled toolbox overflowing with everything you need to construct phenomenal web apps.

But wait, there's more!

Django Full Stack Development with Python isn't just about building websites; it's about empowering you to become a full-stack developer. We'll equip you with the skills to master both the front-end (the user interface, the visual magic users interact with) and the back-end (the powerful engine that drives the application). Imagine the satisfaction of crafting every aspect of a web experience, from the sleek design to the seamless functionality behind the scenes.

Here's a taste of the exhilarating journey you'll embark on:

- **Conquer the Core**: We'll lay the groundwork, teaching you the fundamentals of Python programming and the core concepts of Django. You'll understand how this dynamic duo works together to bring your web app visions to life.
- **Building Blocks of Brilliance**: Delve into the essential components of Django – models, views, and templates. These are the building blocks that structure your application, ensuring organization, clarity, and maintainability.
- **Database Dynamos**: Master the art of data manipulation with Django's Object-Relational Mapper (ORM). This powerful tool allows you to interact with databases seamlessly, storing and retrieving information with ease.

- **Front-End Flair**: We won't neglect the user experience! Explore essential front-end technologies like HTML, CSS,and JavaScript, empowering you to create visually stunning and interactive interfaces.
- **Deployment Dexterity**: So you've built an incredible application – now it's time to share it with the world! We'll guide you through the process of deploying your masterpiece to the web, making it accessible to anyone with an internet connection.

But this book is more than just technical expertise.

We understand that the journey of a web developer is fueled by passion and creativity. We'll provide you with real-world examples, practical exercises, and insightful tips to help you not just learn, but thrive. You'll be challenged, you'll be inspired, and most importantly, you'll have fun!

Django Full Stack Development with Python is your launchpad to a fulfilling career in web development. It's your key to unlocking a world of possibilities, where your imagination becomes the limit. So, are you ready to unleash your inner web architect? Grab your copy today and start building the future of the web, one line of code at a time!

Chapter 1

Why Web Development Matters

Web development matters now more than ever because it's the backbone of the digital world. From simple websites to complex web applications, the demand for web development continues to rise as businesses and individuals rely on the internet for communication, commerce, and entertainment. Let's delve into why web development is crucial, exploring its significance through the lens of Django full-stack development with Python.

Introduction to Django:

Django is a high-level Python web framework that encourages rapid development and clean, pragmatic design. It follows the model-template-views (MTV) architectural pattern and focuses on DRY (Don't Repeat Yourself) principle, which promotes efficiency and maintainability.

Importance of Django in Web Development:

1. Rapid Development: Django's built-in features, such as an ORM (Object-Relational Mapping) system, admin interface, and URL routing, streamline the development process. Developers can quickly build robust web applications with less code, reducing time-to-market.

```python
# Example of URL routing in Django
from django.urls import path
from . import views

urlpatterns = [
    path('articles/', views.article_list),
    path('articles/<int:pk>/', views.article_detail),
]
```

2. Scalability: Django's scalability allows applications to handle increased traffic and data without sacrificing performance. Its ability to support horizontal scaling and integration with caching solutions ensures that web applications remain responsive as they grow.

```python
# Example of scaling with Django
# Use of caching to improve performance
from django.core.cache import cache

def get_articles():
    articles = cache.get('articles')
    if not articles:
```

```
    articles = Article.objects.all()
    cache.set('articles', articles, timeout=3600)  # Cache for 1 hour
    return articles
```

3. Security: Django provides built-in protection against common security threats, such as SQL injection, cross-site scripting (XSS), and cross-site request forgery (CSRF). Its authentication system, middleware, and secure-by-default approach help developers create secure web applications.

```python
# Example of authentication in Django
from django.contrib.auth.decorators import login_required

@login_required
def profile(request):
    # Display user's profile
    ...
```

4. Community and Ecosystem: Django has a vibrant community of developers who contribute to its ecosystem by creating reusable apps, libraries, and documentation. This vast ecosystem accelerates development, promotes best practices, and provides support through forums, conferences, and tutorials.

```python
# Example of using a third-party Django app
# Django Rest Framework for building APIs
from rest_framework.views import APIView
from rest_framework.response import Response

class ArticleList(APIView):
    def get(self, request, format=None):
        articles = Article.objects.all()
        serializer = ArticleSerializer(articles, many=True)
        return Response(serializer.data)
```

5. Cross-platform Compatibility: Django's compatibility with various platforms and databases, including PostgreSQL, MySQL, SQLite, and Oracle, makes it a versatile choice for web development. Developers can deploy Django applications on different operating systems and cloud platforms with ease.

```python
# Example of database integration in Django
# Configuration in settings.py
DATABASES = {
    'default': {
```

```
        'ENGINE': 'django.db.backends.postgresql',
        'NAME': 'mydatabase',
        'USER': 'mydatabaseuser',
        'PASSWORD': 'mypassword',
        'HOST': 'localhost',
        'PORT': '5432',
    }
```

Web development, particularly with Django full-stack development using Python, is essential for building modern, dynamic, and secure web applications. Its features, such as rapid development, scalability, security, vibrant community, and cross-platform compatibility, make it a preferred choice for developers worldwide. As the digital landscape continues to evolve, web development will remain a cornerstone of innovation, enabling businesses and individuals to thrive in the online realm.

Unveiling the Full-Stack Developer: A Journey into Django Full Stack Development with Python

In today's fast-paced digital world, the role of a full-stack developer has become increasingly crucial. Full-stack developers possess the skills and expertise to handle both front-end and back-end development, allowing them to create fully functional web applications from start to finish. In this exploration, we'll delve into the world of full-stack development using Django, a powerful Python web framework, to uncover the responsibilities, challenges, and rewards of being a full-stack developer.

Introduction to Full-Stack Development:

Full-stack development involves working on both the client-side (front end) and server-side (back end) aspects of web development. A full-stack developer is proficient in multiple programming languages, frameworks, and technologies, enabling them to build and maintain all layers of a web application.

The Role of Django in Full-Stack Development:

Django is a high-level Python web framework that simplifies the process of building web applications. It provides a set of tools and libraries for handling common web development tasks, such as URL routing, database integration, and user authentication. As a full-stack developer, leveraging Django allows for rapid development, scalability, and security, making it an ideal choice for building robust web applications.

Front-End Development with Django:

Front-end development focuses on creating the user interface and client-side functionality of a web application. In Django, front-end development typically involves HTML, CSS, JavaScript, and templating engines like Django's built-in template system or popular choices like Jinja2.

```html
<!-- Example of a Django template -->
<!DOCTYPE html>
<html lang="en">
<head>
    <meta charset="UTF-8">
    <title>{{ title }}</title>
</head>
<body>
    <h1>Welcome to {{ title }}</h1>
    <p>{{ content }}</p>
</body>
</html>
```

Front-end development with Django also includes integrating CSS frameworks like Bootstrap for responsive design and JavaScript libraries like jQuery for interactive features.

```html
```

```
<!-- Example of using Bootstrap in Django template -->
{% load static %}
<!DOCTYPE html>
<html lang="en">
<head>
   <meta charset="UTF-8">
   <title>Bootstrap Example</title>
   <link rel="stylesheet" href="{% static 'css/bootstrap.min.css' %}">
   <script src="{% static 'js/bootstrap.min.js' %}"></script>
</head>
<body>
   <div class="container">
      <h1>Welcome to Bootstrap</h1>
      <p>This is a Bootstrap example.</p>
   </div>
</body>
</html>
```
```

**Back-End Development with Django:**

Back-end development involves implementing the server-side logic and database functionality of a web application. In Django, back-end development is primarily done using Python, Django's ORM (Object-Relational Mapping) for database interactions, and
```

Django's built-in authentication system for user management.

```python
# Example of a Django view function
from django.shortcuts import render
from .models import Article

def article_list(request):
    articles = Article.objects.all()
    return render(request, 'articles/article_list.html', {'articles': articles})
```

Django's URL routing mechanism allows developers to map URLs to view functions, enabling clean and organized code structure.

```python
# Example of URL routing in Django
from django.urls import path
from . import views

urlpatterns = [
    path('articles/', views.article_list, name='article_list'),
    path('articles/<int:pk>/', views.article_detail, name='article_detail'),
]
```

```

**Database Integration with Django:**

Django supports multiple databases, including PostgreSQL, MySQL, SQLite, and Oracle. The Django ORM abstracts away the complexities of database interactions, allowing developers to work with database models using Python objects.

```python
# Example of a Django model
from django.db import models

class Article(models.Model):
    title = models.CharField(max_length=100)
    content = models.TextField()
    created_at = models.DateTimeField(auto_now_add=True)
```

Migrations in Django enable developers to propagate changes to the database schema and manage database versioning seamlessly.

```bash
# Example of running Django migrations
python manage.py makemigrations
```
```

python manage.py migrate
```

Full-stack development with Django offers a comprehensive approach to building modern web applications. By combining front-end and back-end development skills, full-stack developers can create dynamic, scalable, and secure web applications that meet the needs of users and businesses alike. With Django's powerful features, extensive documentation, and active community support, the journey of a full-stack developer is filled with opportunities for learning, growth, and innovation in the ever-evolving landscape of web development.

## A Glimpse into the Django & Python Powerhouse: Unleashing the Potential of Full-Stack Development

In the realm of web development, Django and Python stand out as a powerhouse combination, empowering developers to create robust and scalable web applications. From rapid prototyping to deployment, Django's batteries-included philosophy and Python's simplicity and readability make them a preferred choice for full-stack development. Let's take a closer look at how Django and Python work together to unlock the full potential of web development.
```

Introduction to Django and Python:

Django is a high-level Python web framework renowned for its efficiency, scalability, and security. It follows the Model-View-Template (MVT) architectural pattern and promotes the principle of DRY (Don't Repeat Yourself), enabling developers to build complex web applications with ease.

The Power of Python in Web Development:

Python's simplicity and readability make it an ideal language for web development. Its extensive standard library, rich ecosystem of third-party packages, and strong community support contribute to its popularity among developers worldwide. Python's syntax is clean and straightforward, allowing developers to focus on solving problems rather than dealing with syntax complexities.

```python
# Example of Python code
def greet(name):
    return f"Hello, {name}!"

print(greet("World"))
```

Python's dynamic typing and automatic memory management streamline development, while its versatility allows it to be used for a wide range of applications, including web development, data analysis, machine learning, and automation.

Django: Empowering Full-Stack Development:

Django provides a comprehensive set of tools and libraries for building web applications, making it a powerhouse in the world of full-stack development. From URL routing to database integration and user authentication, Django simplifies the development process and promotes best practices.

Rapid Prototyping with Django:

Django's built-in features, such as the admin interface and ORM (Object-Relational Mapping) system, accelerate the prototyping phase of web development. Developers can quickly scaffold CRUD (Create, Read, Update, Delete) operations for database models and focus on refining the application's logic and user experience.

```python
# Example of defining a Django model
```

```python
from django.db import models

class Product(models.Model):
    name = models.CharField(max_length=100)
    price = models.DecimalField(max_digits=10, decimal_places=2)
    description = models.TextField()
```

Scalability with Django:

Django's scalability ensures that web applications can handle increased traffic and data without sacrificing performance. Its support for horizontal scaling and integration with caching solutions like Redis or Memcached allows applications to remain responsive as they grow.

```python
# Example of caching in Django
from django.core.cache import cache

def get_products():
    products = cache.get('products')
    if not products:
        products = Product.objects.all()
        cache.set('products', products, timeout=3600)  # Cache for 1 hour
```

    return products
```

**Security in Django:**

Django prioritizes security and provides built-in protections against common web vulnerabilities, such as SQL injection, cross-site scripting (XSS), and cross-site request forgery (CSRF). Its authentication system, middleware, and secure-by-default approach help developers create secure web applications.

```python
# Example of authentication in Django
from django.contrib.auth.decorators import login_required

@login_required
def profile(request):
    # Display user's profile
    ...
```

Leveraging Django and Python for Full-Stack Development:

In full-stack development with Django and Python, front-end and back-end components work seamlessly
```

together to create dynamic and interactive web applications. Front-end development involves creating the user interface and client-side functionality using HTML, CSS, and JavaScript.

```html
<!-- Example of a Django template -->
<!DOCTYPE html>
<html lang="en">
<head>
   <meta charset="UTF-8">
   <title>{{ title }}</title>
</head>
<body>
   <h1>Welcome to {{ title }}</h1>
   <p>{{ content }}</p>
</body>
</html>
```

Django's templating engine allows developers to generate dynamic content and handle data passed from the back end, enhancing the user experience.

```html
<!-- Example of using Django template tags -->
<!DOCTYPE html>
<html lang="en">
```

```
<head>
    <meta charset="UTF-8">
    <title>Product List</title>
</head>
<body>
    <h1>Product List</h1>
    <ul>
        {% for product in products %}
            <li>{{ product.name }} - ${{ product.price }}</li>
        {% endfor %}
    </ul>
</body>
</html>
```

Django and Python form a formidable powerhouse in the world of full-stack development, empowering developers to create sophisticated and scalable web applications. With Django's robust features and Python's simplicity and versatility, developers can tackle complex web development challenges with confidence. Whether it's rapid prototyping, scalability, security, or seamless integration between front-end and back-end components, Django and Python provide the tools and frameworks needed to bring web application ideas to life. As the digital landscape continues to evolve, Django and

Python remain at the forefront of innovation, driving the future of web development forward.

Chapter 2

Setting Up Your Python Development Environment for Django Full Stack Development

Setting up a robust development environment is crucial for efficient Django full-stack development with Python. In this guide, we'll walk through the steps to set up your Python development environment, including installing Python, setting up a virtual environment, installing Django, and configuring your project structure. Let's dive in!

1. Installing Python:

Python is the backbone of Django development, so the first step is to install Python on your system. You can download the latest version of Python from the official website (https://www.python.org/) or use a package manager like Homebrew (for macOS) or apt (for Linux).

```bash
# macOS with Homebrew
brew install python

# Ubuntu/Debian
```

```
sudo apt update
sudo apt install python3 python3-pip
```

Once Python is installed, verify the installation by running:

```bash
python --version
```

2. Setting Up a Virtual Environment:

A virtual environment is a self-contained directory that houses a Python installation and all the libraries and dependencies required for a specific project. It helps keep project dependencies isolated and prevents conflicts between different projects.

```bash
# Create a virtual environment
python -m venv myenv

# Activate the virtual environment
# macOS/Linux
source myenv/bin/activate

# Windows
```

```
myenv\Scripts\activate
```

3. Installing Django:

With the virtual environment activated, you can now install Django using pip, Python's package manager.

```bash
pip install django
```

Verify that Django is installed by running:

```bash
django-admin --version
```

4. Creating a Django Project:

Now that Django is installed, let's create a new Django project.

```bash
django-admin startproject myproject
```

This command creates a new directory called `myproject`, which contains the basic structure of a Django project.

5. Configuring Your Project Structure:

Inside the `myproject` directory, you'll find the following files and directories:

- `manage.py`: A command-line utility for interacting with Django projects.

- `myproject/`: The Django project directory.

- `__init__.py`: An empty file that tells Python this directory should be considered a Python package.

- `settings.py`: Django project settings, including database configuration, middleware, and installed apps.

- `urls.py`: URL routing configuration for the project.

- `wsgi.py`: WSGI (Web Server Gateway Interface) configuration for deploying the project.

- **`asgi.py`**: ASGI (Asynchronous Server Gateway Interface) configuration for deploying the project asynchronously.

6. Running Your Development Server:

To start the development server and see your Django project in action, navigate to the project directory and run:

```bash
cd myproject
python manage.py runserver
```

This command will start the Django development server, and you can access your project by visiting `http://127.0.0.1:8000` in your web browser.

7. Creating Your First App:

In Django, an app is a web application that performs a specific function within a project. Let's create our first app called `myapp`.

```bash
python manage.py startapp myapp
```

This command will create a new directory called `myapp`, which contains the files and directories for our app.

8. Configuring Your App:

Inside the `myapp` directory, you'll find the following files and directories:

- `__init__.py`: An empty file that tells Python this directory should be considered a Python package.

- `admin.py`: Configuration for registering models with the Django admin interface.

- `apps.py`: Configuration for the app itself.

- `models.py`: Database models for the app.

- `views.py`: View functions for handling HTTP requests.

- `urls.py`: URL routing configuration for the app.

- `tests.py`: Unit tests for the app.

9. Integrating Your App with the Project:

To integrate your app with the project, you need to add it to the `INSTALLED_APPS` list in the `settings.py` file of your project.

```python
# settings.py

INSTALLED_APPS = [
    ...
    'myapp',
    ...
]
```

10. Creating a Model:

Models in Django represent the structure of your database. Let's define a simple model for our `myapp` app.

```python
# models.py

from django.db import models

class MyModel(models.Model):
```

```
name = models.CharField(max_length=100)
description = models.TextField()
created_at = models.DateTimeField(auto_now_add=True)

def __str__(self):
    return self.name
```

11. Running Migrations:

Once you've defined your models, you need to create database tables for them. Django provides a migration system to manage changes to your database schema.

```bash
python manage.py makemigrations
python manage.py migrate
```

12. Creating Views and URLs:

Views in Django are Python functions or classes that take HTTP requests and return HTTP responses. Let's create a simple view for our `myapp` app.

```python
# views.py
```

```python
from django.shortcuts import render
from .models import MyModel

def index(request):
    objects = MyModel.objects.all()
    return render(request, 'myapp/index.html', {'objects': objects})
```

Next, we'll define a URL pattern to map the view to a URL.

```python
# urls.py (inside the app directory)

from django.urls import path
from . import views

urlpatterns = [
    path('', views.index, name='index'),
]
```

13. Creating Templates:

Templates in Django are HTML files that contain placeholders for dynamically generated content. Let's create a template to render the data from our view.

```html
<!-- index.html (inside the templates directory of your app) -->

<!DOCTYPE html>
<html lang="en">
<head>
    <meta charset="UTF-8">
    <title>My App</title>
</head>
<body>
    <h1>My App</h1>
    <ul>
        {% for object in objects %}
            <li>{{ object.name }} - {{ object.description }}</li>
        {% endfor %}
    </ul>
</body>
</html>
```

14. Running Your Development Server Again:

Finally, start your development server again to see your changes in action.

```bash
python manage.py runserver
```

Visit `http://127.0.0.1:8000` in your web browser to view your Django app with the newly added functionality.

Congratulations! You've successfully set up your Python development environment for Django full-stack development and created a simple Django app. From installing Python and Django to configuring your project structure, creating apps, defining models, and writing views and templates, you've covered the essential steps to get started with Django development. As you continue your journey, explore Django's rich ecosystem of libraries, tools, and documentation to build even more sophisticated web applications. Happy coding!

Demystifying Variables, Data Types, and Operators in Python

In Python, variables, data types, and operators form the building blocks of programming. Understanding these fundamental concepts is essential for Django full-stack development, as they enable developers to manipulate data, perform calculations, and build dynamic web applications. Let's demystify variables, data types, and operators in Python and explore how they are used in the context of Django full-stack development.

1. Variables:

Variables are containers used to store data values. In Python, variables are created when a value is assigned to them using the assignment operator (`=`). Variables can store different types of data, such as numbers, strings, lists, or objects.

```python
# Example of assigning values to variables
name = "John"
age = 30
is_student = True
```

In Django development, variables are commonly used to store data retrieved from the database, user input, or calculations performed within the application.

```python
# Example of using variables in Django view function
from django.shortcuts import render
```

```
def index(request):
    username = "John"
    user_age = 30
    return render(request, 'index.html', {'username': username, 'user_age': user_age})
```
```

**2. Data Types:**

Data types define the type of data that can be stored in a variable. Python supports several built-in data types, including:

- **int**: Integer numbers (e.g., 1, 2, -3).

- **float**: Floating-point numbers (e.g., 3.14, -0.5).

- **str**: Strings of characters (e.g., "hello", 'world').

- **bool**: Boolean values (True or False).

- **list**: Ordered collection of items (e.g., [1, 2, 3]).

- **tuple**: Immutable ordered collection of items (e.g., (1, 2, 3)).
```

- **dict**: Collection of key-value pairs (e.g., {'name': 'John', 'age': 30}).

```python
# Example of different data types
name = "John"  # str
age = 30  # int
is_student = True  # bool
grades = [90, 85, 95]  # list
```

In Django development, understanding data types is crucial for handling user input, processing data from the database, and passing data between different parts of the application.

3. Operators:

Operators are symbols or keywords used to perform operations on variables and values. Python supports various types of operators, including arithmetic, comparison, logical, assignment, and bitwise operators.

Arithmetic Operators:

Arithmetic operators are used to perform mathematical operations such as addition, subtraction, multiplication, and division.

```python
# Example of arithmetic operators
x = 10
y = 3

addition = x + y  # 13
subtraction = x - y  # 7
multiplication = x * y  # 30
division = x / y  # 3.3333333333333335
```

Comparison Operators:

Comparison operators are used to compare the values of variables and return Boolean values (True or False).

```python
# Example of comparison operators
x = 10
y = 3

greater_than = x > y  # True
less_than = x < y  # False
equal_to = x == y  # False
not_equal_to = x != y  # True
```

Logical Operators:

Logical operators are used to combine multiple conditions and evaluate them as a single condition.

```python
# Example of logical operators
x = 10
y = 3
z = 5

logical_and = (x > y) and (y > z)  # True
logical_or = (x > y) or (y < z)  # True
logical_not = not (x == y)  # True
```

Assignment Operators:

Assignment operators are used to assign values to variables. They combine the assignment (`=`) operator with other arithmetic or logical operators.

```python
# Example of assignment operators
x = 10
x += 5  # Equivalent to x = x + 5 (x is now 15)
```

Bitwise Operators:

Bitwise operators are used to perform bitwise operations on binary representations of numbers.

```python
# Example of bitwise operators
x = 5  # 101 in binary
y = 3  # 011 in binary

bitwise_and = x & y  # 1 (001 in binary)
bitwise_or = x | y  # 7 (111 in binary)
bitwise_xor = x ^ y  # 6 (110 in binary)
bitwise_not = ~x  # -6 (-101 in binary)
```

Understanding variables, data types, and operators is essential for Django full-stack development, as they form the foundation of programming logic and data manipulation. By mastering these fundamental concepts, developers can write more efficient and effective code, build dynamic web applications, and solve complex problems with ease. Whether it's storing data in variables, working with different data types, or performing operations using operators, these concepts play a crucial role in every aspect of Django development. So, keep practicing and exploring, and continue to deepen your understanding of Python programming for Django full-stack development. Happy coding!

Mastering Control Flow with Conditional Statements and Loops in Python

Control flow structures such as conditional statements and loops are fundamental tools for directing the flow of execution in Python programs. In the context of Django full-stack development, mastering these control flow structures enables developers to create dynamic and interactive web applications. Let's delve into conditional statements and loops, explore their syntax, and see how they are used in Django development.

1. Conditional Statements:

Conditional statements allow developers to execute different blocks of code based on certain conditions. In Python, conditional statements are implemented using the `if`, `elif`, and `else` keywords.

Example of `if` statement:

```python
# Example of if statement
x = 10
```

```python
if x > 0:
    print("x is positive")
```

Example of `if-else` statement:

```python
# Example of if-else statement
x = -5

if x > 0:
    print("x is positive")
else:
    print("x is non-positive")
```

Example of `if-elif-else` statement:

```python
# Example of if-elif-else statement
x = 0

if x > 0:
    print("x is positive")
elif x == 0:
    print("x is zero")
else:
    print("x is negative")
```

```

In Django development, conditional statements are commonly used for handling user input, validating data, and controlling the flow of execution based on various conditions.

**2. Loops:**

Loops allow developers to iterate over a sequence of elements and perform repetitive tasks efficiently. Python supports two types of loops: `for` loops and `while` loops.

**Example of `for` loop:**

```python
# Example of for loop
fruits = ["apple", "banana", "cherry"]

for fruit in fruits:
    print(fruit)
```

Example of `while` loop:

```python
# Example of while loop
```
```

```
count = 0

while count < 5:
    print(count)
    count += 1
```

In Django development, loops are frequently used for iterating over lists, querying database objects, and generating dynamic content for web pages.

3. Control Flow within Views:

In Django, views are Python functions or classes that handle HTTP requests and return HTTP responses. Control flow structures such as conditional statements and loops are often used within views to control the logic of web applications.

Example of conditional statements in views:

```python
# Example of conditional statements in Django views
from django.shortcuts import render

def index(request):
    is_authenticated = request.user.is_authenticated
```

```
    if is_authenticated:
        return render(request, 'dashboard.html')
    else:
        return render(request, 'login.html')
```

Example of loops in views:

```python
# Example of loops in Django views
from django.shortcuts import render
from .models import Product

def product_list(request):
    products = Product.objects.all()
    return render(request, 'product_list.html', {'products': products})
```

In the above examples, conditional statements are used to determine whether to render the dashboard or login page based on the user's authentication status. Loops are used to iterate over a list of products retrieved from the database and render them on the product list page.

4. Control Flow within Templates:

In Django, templates are HTML files that contain placeholders for dynamically generated content. Control flow structures such as conditional statements and loops can be used within templates to conditionally display content or iterate over lists.

Example of conditional statements in templates:

```html
<!-- Example of conditional statements in Django templates -->
{% if user.is_authenticated %}
    <p>Welcome, {{ user.username }}!</p>
{% else %}
    <p>Please log in to continue.</p>
{% endif %}
```

Example of loops in templates:

```html
<!-- Example of loops in Django templates -->
<ul>
    {% for product in products %}
        <li>{{ product.name }} - ${{ product.price }}</li>
    {% endfor %}
</ul>
```

In the above examples, conditional statements are used in the template to display a welcome message if the user is authenticated and a login prompt if the user is not authenticated. Loops are used to iterate over a list of products and display each product's name and price.

Mastering control flow with conditional statements and loops is essential for effective Django full-stack development. These control flow structures enable developers to write logic that responds dynamically to user input, handles data efficiently, and generates dynamic content for web pages. By understanding the syntax and usage of conditional statements and loops, developers can build interactive and engaging web applications that meet the needs of users and businesses alike. So, keep practicing and exploring the power of control flow in Django development, and unlock the full potential of your web applications. Happy coding!

Building Reusable Code with Functions in Django Full Stack Development

Functions play a crucial role in Django full-stack development by enabling developers to encapsulate logic, promote code reusability, and maintain a modular codebase. In this guide, we'll explore how to create and use functions in Django applications, leveraging their power to build scalable and maintainable web applications.

1. Creating Functions:

Functions in Python are defined using the `def` keyword followed by the function name and parameters, if any. In Django development, functions are commonly used within views, utility modules, and template tags to encapsulate specific tasks or operations.

Example of a simple function:

```python
# Example of a simple function
def greet(name):
    return f"Hello, {name}!"
```

Example of a function with parameters:

```python
# Example of a function with parameters
def add(x, y):
    return x + y
```

2. Using Functions in Views:

In Django, views are Python functions or classes that handle HTTP requests and return HTTP responses. Functions are often used within views to encapsulate business logic, database queries, and other operations.

Example of using a function in a view:

```python
# Example of using a function in a Django view
from django.shortcuts import render

def index(request):
    message = get_greeting("John")
    return render(request, 'index.html', {'message': message})

def get_greeting(name):
    return f"Hello, {name}!"
```

3. Organizing Functions in Utility Modules:

To promote code organization and reusability, functions can be organized into utility modules within a Django application. Utility modules contain functions that perform specific tasks or operations and can be imported into views, models, or other modules as needed.

Example of a utility module with functions:

```python
# Example of a utility module with functions
# utils.py

def add(x, y):
    return x + y

def subtract(x, y):
    return x - y
```

Example of importing and using functions from a utility module:

```python
# Example of importing and using functions from a utility module
from .utils import add, subtract

result1 = add(5, 3)
result2 = subtract(10, 5)
```

4. Using Functions in Template Tags:

In Django, template tags are custom template filters or functions that can be used within HTML templates to perform operations or display dynamic content. Functions can be defined as template tags to encapsulate complex logic or data processing.

Example of defining a custom template tag as a function:

```python
# Example of defining a custom template tag as a function
# my_tags.py

from django import template

register = template.Library()

@register.simple_tag
def get_greeting(name):
    return f"Hello, {name}!"
```

Example of using a custom template tag in a template:

```html
```

```
<!-- Example of using a custom template tag in a Django template -->
{% load my_tags %}

<p>{{ user_name|get_greeting }}</p>
```

5. Best Practices for Writing Functions:

When writing functions in Django full-stack development, it's important to follow best practices to ensure code readability, maintainability, and scalability.

- **Use meaningful names:** Choose descriptive names for functions that accurately convey their purpose and functionality.

- **Keep functions small and focused:** Divide complex tasks into smaller, more manageable functions with a single responsibility.

- **Follow the DRY principle:** Don't Repeat Yourself. Avoid duplicating code by encapsulating reusable logic into functions.

- **Document functions:** Provide clear and concise documentation for functions to explain their purpose, parameters, and return values.

- **Test functions:** Write unit tests for functions to ensure they behave as expected and handle edge cases correctly.

Functions are a powerful tool in Django full-stack development for encapsulating logic, promoting code reusability, and maintaining a modular codebase. By creating well-organized and purposeful functions, developers can build scalable and maintainable web applications that meet the needs of users and businesses. Whether it's encapsulating business logic in views, organizing utility functions into modules, defining custom template tags, or following best practices for writing functions, mastering the art of function-based development is essential for success in Django development. So, keep practicing and exploring the power of functions in Django, and unlock the full potential of your web applications. Happy coding!

Chapter 3

Understanding the MVC Architecture in Django Full Stack Development

The Model-View-Controller (MVC) architecture is a software design pattern commonly used in web development to separate the concerns of an application into three interconnected components: the Model, the View, and the Controller. In this guide, we'll explore how the MVC architecture applies to Django full-stack development, understand the roles of each component, and see how they work together to create dynamic web applications.

1. Model:

The Model component represents the application's data and business logic. In Django, models are Python classes that define the structure and behavior of the application's data, including database tables, fields, and relationships.

Example of a Django model:

```python
# Example of a Django model
from django.db import models
```

```
class Product(models.Model):
    name = models.CharField(max_length=100)
    price = models.DecimalField(max_digits=10, decimal_places=2)
    description = models.TextField()

    def __str__(self):
        return self.name
```

In the above example, the `Product` model defines a database table with fields for storing product names, prices, and descriptions. The `__str__` method specifies how instances of the model should be displayed in the Django admin interface and other contexts.

2. View:

The View component is responsible for presenting the application's data to the user and handling user interactions. In Django, views are Python functions or classes that receive HTTP requests, perform any necessary processing or data retrieval, and return HTTP responses, typically in the form of rendered HTML templates.

Example of a Django view function:

```python
# Example of a Django view function
from django.shortcuts import render
from .models import Product

def product_list(request):
    products = Product.objects.all()
    return render(request, 'product_list.html', {'products': products})
```

In the above example, the `product_list` view function retrieves all products from the database using the `Product` model and passes them to a template named `product_list.html` for rendering. The rendered HTML is then returned as an HTTP response to the client.

3. Controller:

The Controller component acts as an intermediary between the Model and the View, handling user input, processing requests, and coordinating interactions between the Model and the View. In Django, the Controller is typically represented by the URL routing mechanism and the view functions or classes that are associated with specific URLs.

Example of URL routing in Django:

```python
# Example of URL routing in Django
from django.urls import path
from .views import product_list

urlpatterns = [
    path('products/', product_list, name='product_list'),
]
```

In the above example, the URL pattern `/products/` is mapped to the `product_list` view function. When a user navigates to the `/products/` URL, Django invokes the `product_list` view function to handle the request and return the appropriate response.

4. How MVC Works in Django:

In Django, the MVC architecture is implemented as follows:

- **Model**: Django models represent the application's data and business logic. They define the structure of the database and provide an interface for interacting with data.

- **View**: Django views receive HTTP requests, retrieve data from the database using models, and render HTML templates to present the data to the user.

- **Controller**: In Django, the URL routing mechanism serves as the Controller component. It maps URLs to view functions or classes, allowing for the processing of user requests and the coordination of interactions between the Model and the View.

The Model-View-Controller (MVC) architecture is a powerful design pattern for organizing code and separating concerns in web applications. In Django full-stack development, the MVC architecture is implemented through models, views, and URL routing, enabling developers to build scalable, maintainable, and modular web applications. By understanding the roles of each component and how they work together, developers can create dynamic and interactive web applications that meet the needs of users and businesses. So, keep exploring the MVC architecture in Django, and leverage its power to build powerful and efficient web applications. Happy coding!

Installing and Configuring Django for Full Stack Development

Django is a high-level Python web framework that facilitates rapid development and clean, pragmatic design. It follows the Model-View-Controller (MVC) architectural pattern, known in Django as Model-View-Template (MVT), which helps developers build scalable and maintainable web applications. In this guide, we'll walk through the process of installing and configuring Django for full-stack development, including setting up a development environment, creating a new project, and configuring project settings.

1. Installing Django:

Before we can start using Django, we need to install it along with its dependencies. We can do this using Python's package manager, pip.

```bash
pip install django
```

This command will install the latest version of Django available in the Python Package Index (PyPI) on your system.

2. Creating a New Django Project:

Once Django is installed, we can create a new Django project using the `django-admin` command-line utility.

```bash
django-admin startproject myproject
```

This command will create a new directory called `myproject`, which contains the basic structure of a Django project.

3. Project Structure:

Inside the `myproject` directory, you'll find the following files and directories:

- `manage.py`: A command-line utility for interacting with Django projects.

- `myproject/`: The Django project directory.

- `__init__.py`: An empty file that tells Python this directory should be considered a Python package.

- `settings.py`: Django project settings, including database configuration, middleware, and installed apps.

- `urls.py`: URL routing configuration for the project.

- `wsgi.py`: WSGI (Web Server Gateway Interface) configuration for deploying the project.

- `asgi.py`: ASGI (Asynchronous Server Gateway Interface) configuration for deploying the project asynchronously.

4. Running the Development Server:

To start the development server and see your Django project in action, navigate to the project directory and run:

```bash
cd myproject
python manage.py runserver
```

This command will start the Django development server, and you can access your project by visiting `http://127.0.0.1:8000` in your web browser.

5. Creating an App:

In Django, an app is a web application that performs a specific function within a project. Let's create our first app called `myapp`.

```bash
python manage.py startapp myapp
```

This command will create a new directory called `myapp`, which contains the files and directories for our app.

6. Integrating the App with the Project:

To integrate your app with the project, you need to add it to the `INSTALLED_APPS` list in the `settings.py` file of your project.

```python
# settings.py

INSTALLED_APPS = [
    ...
    'myapp',
    ...
```

```
]
```

7. Creating a Model:

Models in Django represent the structure of your database. Let's define a simple model for our `myapp` app.

```python
# models.py (inside the app directory)

from django.db import models

class MyModel(models.Model):
    name = models.CharField(max_length=100)
    description = models.TextField()
    created_at = models.DateTimeField(auto_now_add=True)

    def __str__(self):
        return self.name
```

8. Running Migrations:

Once you've defined your models, you need to create database tables for them. Django provides a migration system to manage changes to your database schema.

```bash
python manage.py makemigrations
python manage.py migrate
```

9. Creating Views and URLs:

Views in Django are Python functions or classes that take HTTP requests and return HTTP responses. Let's create a simple view for our `myapp` app.

```python
# views.py (inside the app directory)

from django.shortcuts import render
from .models import MyModel

def index(request):
    objects = MyModel.objects.all()
    return render(request, 'index.html', {'objects': objects})
```

Next, we'll define a URL pattern to map the view to a URL.

```python
# urls.py (inside the app directory)

from django.urls import path
from . import views

urlpatterns = [
    path('', views.index, name='index'),
]
```

10. Creating Templates:

Templates in Django are HTML files that contain placeholders for dynamically generated content. Let's create a template to render the data from our view.

```html
<!-- index.html (inside the templates directory of your app) -->

<!DOCTYPE html>
<html lang="en">
<head>
    <meta charset="UTF-8">
    <title>My App</title>
</head>
```

```
<body>
    <h1>My App</h1>
    <ul>
       {% for object in objects %}
          <li>{{ object.name }} - {{ object.description }}</li>
       {% endfor %}
    </ul>
</body>
</html>
```

Congratulations! You've successfully installed and configured Django for full-stack development and created a simple Django app. From creating a new project and integrating apps to defining models, views, URLs, and templates, you've covered the essential steps to get started with Django development. As you continue your journey, explore Django's rich ecosystem of libraries, tools, and documentation to build even more sophisticated web applications. Happy coding!

Creating Your First Django Project: Let's Get Coding!

Django is a high-level Python web framework that encourages rapid development and clean, pragmatic design. It's built by experienced developers and used by some of the world's largest and most popular websites.

Django handles much of the hassle of web development, so you can focus on writing your app without needing to reinvent the wheel.

In this tutorial, we'll walk through the process of creating your first Django project. By the end, you'll have a basic understanding of how Django works and how to create a simple web application using it.

Setting Up Your Development Environment:

Before we dive into coding, let's make sure you have Django installed on your machine. You'll also need Python installed, preferably version 3.6 or higher.

First, create a new directory for your project:

```bash
mkdir myproject
cd myproject
```

Next, let's set up a virtual environment to isolate our project dependencies:

```bash
python3 -m venv myenv
```

Activate the virtual environment:

```bash
source myenv/bin/activate
```

Now, let's install Django:

```bash
pip install django
```

Creating Your Django Project:

With Django installed, we can now create our first project. In your terminal, run the following command:

```bash
django-admin startproject myproject
```

This will create a new directory called `myproject` with the following structure:

```
myproject/
    manage.py
```

```
myproject/
    __init__.py
    settings.py
    urls.py
    asgi.py
    wsgi.py
```

Let's briefly explain each file:

- `manage.py`: A command-line utility that lets you interact with your Django project.

- `myproject/`: The Python package for your project.

- `__init__.py`: An empty file that tells Python this directory should be considered a Python package.

- `settings.py`: Configuration settings for your Django project.

- `urls.py`: URL declarations for your project.

- `asgi.py` and `wsgi.py`: Entry points for ASGI and WSGI, which are the interface between Django and your web server.

Starting the Development Server:

Now that our project is set up, let's start the development server. Navigate to the `myproject` directory and run:

```bash
python manage.py runserver
```

You should see output indicating that the development server is running. Open your web browser and navigate to `http://127.0.0.1:8000/`. You should see the Django welcome page, indicating that everything is set up correctly.

Creating Your First App:

In Django, a project is made up of one or more apps. Each app is a self-contained package that handles a specific aspect of your project, such as managing users or handling blog posts.

Let's create our first app. In your terminal, navigate to the `myproject` directory and run:

```bash
python manage.py startapp myapp
```

```

This will create a new directory called `myapp` with the following structure:

```
myapp/
    __init__.py
    admin.py
    apps.py
    migrations/
        __init__.py
    models.py
    tests.py
    views.py
```

Let's briefly explain each file:

- `__init__.py`: An empty file that tells Python this directory should be considered a Python package.

- `admin.py`: Configuration for the Django admin interface.

- `apps.py`: Configuration for the app itself.
```

- `**migrations/**`: Directory for database migrations.

- `**models.py**`: Defines the data models for your app.

- `**tests.py**`: Contains test cases for your app.

- `**views.py**`: Defines the views, which handle HTTP requests and return responses.

Defining Models:

Now that we have our app set up, let's define a simple data model. Open `myapp/models.py` and add the following code:

```python
from django.db import models

class Post(models.Model):
    title = models.CharField(max_length=100)
    content = models.TextField()
    created_at = models.DateTimeField(auto_now_add=True)

    def __str__(self):
        return self.title
```

This defines a `Post` model with three fields: `title`, `content`, and `created_at`. The `__str__` method specifies how instances of the model should be displayed in the Django admin interface and other contexts.

Creating Database Tables:

Next, let's create database tables for our models. Run the following command in your terminal:

```bash
python manage.py makemigrations
python manage.py migrate
```

This will generate a migration file based on the changes to your models and apply those changes to the database.

Registering Models with the Admin Interface:

To make it easier to manage our data, let's register the `Post` model with the Django admin interface. Open `myapp/admin.py` and add the following code:

```python
from django.contrib import admin
from .models import Post
```

```
admin.site.register(Post)
```

Now, if you run the development server and navigate to `http://127.0.0.1:8000/admin/`, you'll be prompted to log in. After logging in, you should see the `Posts` section, where you can add, edit, and delete posts.

Creating Views:

With our models set up, let's create some views to display our data. Open `myapp/views.py` and add the following code:

```python
from django.shortcuts import render
from .models import Post

def post_list(request):
    posts = Post.objects.all()
    return render(request, 'myapp/post_list.html', {'posts': posts})
```

This defines a `post_list` view that retrieves all posts from the database and passes them to a template called `post_list.html`.

Creating Templates:

Next, let's create the `post_list.html` template. Create a new directory called `templates` inside the `myapp` directory, and then create a new file called `post_list.html` with the following content:

```html
<!DOCTYPE html>
<html>
<head>
    <title>My Blog</title>
</head>
<body>
    <h1>My Blog</h1>
    {% for post in posts %}
        <div>
            <h2>{{ post.title }}</h2>
            <p>{{ post.content }}</p>
            <p>Created at: {{ post.created_at }}</p>
        </div>
    {% endfor %}
</body>
</html>
```

This template displays a list of posts, including their titles, content, and creation dates.

Mapping URLs to Views:

Finally, let's map URLs to our views. Open `myproject/urls.py` and replace its contents with the following code:

```python
from django.contrib import admin
from django.urls import path
from myapp import views

urlpatterns = [
    path('admin/', admin.site.urls),
    path('', views.post_list, name='post_list'),
]
```

This maps the root URL to the `post_list` view we defined earlier.

Congratulations! You've just created your first Django project and built a simple web application with it. This tutorial only scratches the surface of what Django can do, but hopefully, it gives you a good starting point for further exploration. Happy coding!

Chapter 4

The Backbone: Models and Object-Relational Mapping (ORM)

Designing Your Data Structure with Models in Django

In Django, models are Python classes that represent the structure of your application's data. They encapsulate the fields and behaviors of the data you're storing, making it easy to work with databases without having to write SQL queries directly.

In this tutorial, we'll explore how to design your data structure using models in Django. We'll cover defining models, specifying fields, creating relationships between models, and more.

Defining Models:

To define a model in Django, you create a Python class that inherits from `django.db.models.Model`. Each attribute of the class represents a database field, and each instance of the class represents a record in the database.

Let's start by creating a simple model for a blog post. In your Django app directory, typically named `myapp`, open the `models.py` file and add the following code:

```python
from django.db import models

class Post(models.Model):
    title = models.CharField(max_length=200)
    content = models.TextField()
    created_at = models.DateTimeField(auto_now_add=True)
```

In this example, we've defined a `Post` model with three fields: `title`, `content`, and `created_at`. The `CharField` represents a character field, `TextField` represents a large text field, and `DateTimeField` represents a date and time field.

Specifying Fields:

Django provides a wide range of field types to cover different data types and database requirements. Here are some commonly used field types:

- `CharField`: A field for storing a fixed-length string.

- `TextField`: A field for storing large amounts of text.

- `IntegerField`, `FloatField`, `DecimalField`: Fields for storing numerical data.

- `DateField`, `DateTimeField`, `TimeField`: Fields for storing date and time information.

- `BooleanField`: A field for storing boolean (True/False) values.

- `ForeignKey`: A field for creating many-to-one relationships between models.

- `ManyToManyField`: A field for creating many-to-many relationships between models.

Creating Relationships Between Models:

One of the powerful features of Django is its ability to create relationships between models. Let's extend our blog example to include a `Comment` model that is related to the `Post` model:

```python
class Comment(models.Model):
```

```
    post = models.ForeignKey(Post,
on_delete=models.CASCADE)
    author = models.CharField(max_length=100)
    content = models.TextField()
    created_at = models.DateTimeField(auto_now_add=True)
```

In this example, we've defined a `Comment` model with a `ForeignKey` field called `post`, which establishes a many-to-one relationship between comments and posts. The `on_delete=models.CASCADE` argument specifies that if a post is deleted, all associated comments should also be deleted.

Creating Model Methods:

Models in Django can also include methods that perform operations on model instances. For example, let's add a method to our `Post` model that returns a truncated version of the post content:

```python
class Post(models.Model):
    title = models.CharField(max_length=200)
    content = models.TextField()
    created_at = models.DateTimeField(auto_now_add=True)
```

```
    def short_content(self):
        return self.content[:100] + '...'
```

Now, you can call the `short_content` method on a `Post` instance to get a truncated version of the post content.

Registering Models with the Admin Interface:

To interact with your models in the Django admin interface, you need to register them with the admin site. Open the `admin.py` file in your app directory and add the following code:

```python
from django.contrib import admin
from .models import Post, Comment

admin.site.register(Post)
admin.site.register(Comment)
```

Now, you'll be able to manage posts and comments directly from the Django admin interface.

Running Migrations:

Before you can use your models, you need to create database tables for them. Django provides a migration system that automatically generates SQL to create, modify, or delete database tables based on changes to your models.

To create and apply migrations, run the following commands in your terminal:

```bash
python manage.py makemigrations
python manage.py migrate
```

This will create migration files based on the changes to your models and apply those changes to the database.

Querying Data:

Once your models are set up and your database tables are created, you can start querying data using Django's ORM (Object-Relational Mapping) system. Here are some examples of common queries:

```python
# Get all posts
posts = Post.objects.all()
```

```
# Get a specific post by its primary key
post = Post.objects.get(pk=1)

# Filter posts by a specific condition
filtered_posts = Post.objects.filter(title__icontains='django')

# Create a new post
new_post = Post(title='New Post', content='Lorem ipsum...')
new_post.save()

# Update an existing post
post.title = 'Updated Title'
post.save()

# Delete a post
post.delete()
```

Django's ORM translates these Pythonic queries into SQL queries, allowing you to interact with your database using familiar Python syntax.

Designing your data structure with models is a fundamental aspect of Django development. By defining models, specifying fields, creating relationships between models, and registering them with the admin interface, you can create powerful and flexible web applications with Django. Additionally, Django's migration system and ORM make it easy to work with databases without needing to write raw SQL queries.

Interacting with Databases Using Django's ORM

Django is a powerful web framework for building robust web applications using Python. One of its key features is the Object-Relational Mapping (ORM) layer, which provides an abstraction over the database, allowing developers to interact with the database using Python objects. In this tutorial, we'll explore how to interact with databases using Django's ORM.

Setting Up Django Project:

First, let's create a new Django project and app. Open your terminal and run the following commands:

```bash
django-admin startproject myproject
cd myproject
python manage.py startapp myapp
```

Next, add 'myapp' to the `INSTALLED_APPS` list in the `settings.py` file of your project.

Defining Models:

Models in Django are Python classes that represent database tables. Let's define a simple model for a blog post in `models.py`:

```python
from django.db import models

class Post(models.Model):
    title = models.CharField(max_length=100)
    content = models.TextField()
    published_date = models.DateTimeField(auto_now_add=True)
```

After defining the model, run the following command to create the corresponding database table:

```bash
python manage.py makemigrations
python manage.py migrate
```

Interacting with the Database:

Now that we have our model set up, let's see how we can interact with the database using Django's ORM.

1. Creating Objects:

```python
from myapp.models import Post

# Create a new post
post = Post.objects.create(title='First Post', content='This is the content of my first post.')
```

2. Querying Objects:

```python
# Retrieve all posts
all_posts = Post.objects.all()

# Retrieve a specific post by its primary key
post = Post.objects.get(pk=1)

# Filter posts based on certain criteria
filtered_posts = Post.objects.filter(title__icontains='django')

# Chain multiple filters
```

```
filtered_posts = Post.objects.filter(title__icontains='django').filter(published_date__year=2024)
```

3. Updating Objects:

```python
# Update a specific post
post = Post.objects.get(pk=1)
post.title = 'Updated Title'
post.save()
```

4. Deleting Objects:

```python
# Delete a specific post
post = Post.objects.get(pk=1)
post.delete()

# Delete all posts that match a certain criteria
Post.objects.filter(published_date__year=2023).delete()
```

5. Aggregations:

```python
```

```
from django.db.models import Count

# Count the number of posts
num_posts = Post.objects.count()

# Get the average length of post content
avg_content_length =
Post.objects.aggregate(avg_length=Avg('content'))
```

Django's ORM provides a convenient way to interact with databases using Python, abstracting away the complexities of SQL queries. In this tutorial, we've covered the basics of defining models, creating, querying, updating, and deleting objects, as well as performing aggregations. With Django's ORM, you can build powerful web applications with ease.

Performing CRUD Operations (Create, Read, Update, Delete) with Ease

Performing CRUD operations (Create, Read, Update, Delete) is a fundamental aspect of building web applications. In this guide, I'll walk you through how to perform CRUD operations with ease using Django, a high-level Python web framework, for full-stack development.

Setting Up Django Project

First, ensure you have Django installed. If not, you can install it via pip:

```bash
pip install django
```

Now, let's create a new Django project:

```bash
django-admin startproject myproject
```

Navigate into the project directory:

```bash
cd myproject
```

Creating a Django App

Django apps are components of a Django project that handle specific functionality. Let's create a new app called 'myapp':

```bash
python manage.py startapp myapp
```

```

Next, we need to register our app in the settings.py file of the project:

```python
INSTALLED_APPS = [
    ...
    'myapp',
    ...
]
```

Defining Models

Models in Django represent the structure of the data and are used to interact with the database. Open the models.py file inside the 'myapp' directory and define your models:

```python
from django.db import models

class MyModel(models.Model):
    name = models.CharField(max_length=100)
    description = models.TextField()

    def __str__(self):

```
    return self.name
```

Migrating Database Changes

After defining models, we need to create migrations and apply them to the database:

```bash
python manage.py makemigrations
python manage.py migrate
```

Performing CRUD Operations

Create Operation (Adding Data)

To create a new instance of the model, we can use the Django ORM (Object-Relational Mapping):

```python
from myapp.models import MyModel

# Create
new_instance = MyModel(name="New Instance", description="This is a new instance.")
new_instance.save()
```

Read Operation (Retrieving Data)

To retrieve data from the database, we can use various query methods provided by Django:

```python
# Read (Retrieve all instances)
all_instances = MyModel.objects.all()

# Retrieve a specific instance by ID
instance = MyModel.objects.get(id=1)

# Filtering instances
filtered_instances = MyModel.objects.filter(name__icontains="instance")
```

Update Operation (Modifying Data)

To update an existing instance, retrieve it from the database and modify its attributes:

```python
# Update
instance = MyModel.objects.get(id=1)
instance.name = "Updated Instance"
instance.save()
```

```

## Delete Operation (Removing Data)

To delete an instance, simply call the delete method on the instance:

```python
# Delete
instance = MyModel.objects.get(id=1)
instance.delete()
```

Views and Templates (Optional)

To interact with these CRUD operations via a web interface, we can define views and templates.

Views (views.py)

```python
from django.shortcuts import render, redirect
from myapp.models import MyModel

def index(request):
    instances = MyModel.objects.all()
    return render(request, 'index.html', {'instances': instances})
```
```

```
def create(request):
    if request.method == 'POST':
        name = request.POST.get('name')
        description = request.POST.get('description')
        MyModel.objects.create(name=name, description=description)
        return redirect('index')
    return render(request, 'create.html')

def update(request, id):
    instance = MyModel.objects.get(id=id)
    if request.method == 'POST':
        instance.name = request.POST.get('name')
        instance.description = request.POST.get('description')
        instance.save()
        return redirect('index')
    return render(request, 'update.html', {'instance': instance})

def delete(request, id):
    instance = MyModel.objects.get(id=id)
    instance.delete()
    return redirect('index')
```
```

## **Templates (HTML files)**
```

Create HTML files in the 'templates' directory:

- index.html
```html
<!DOCTYPE html>
<html lang="en">
<head>
    <meta charset="UTF-8">
    <title>CRUD Operations</title>
</head>
<body>
    <h1>Instances</h1>
    <ul>
        {% for instance in instances %}
        <li>{{ instance.name }}</li>
        {% endfor %}
    </ul>
</body>
</html>
```

- create.html
```html
<!DOCTYPE html>
<html lang="en">
<head>
    <meta charset="UTF-8">
```

```html
    <title>Create Instance</title>
</head>
<body>
    <h1>Create Instance</h1>
    <form method="post">
        {% csrf_token %}
        <input type="text" name="name" placeholder="Name"><br>
        <textarea name="description" placeholder="Description"></textarea><br>
        <input type="submit" value="Create">
    </form>
</body>
</html>
```

- update.html
```html
<!DOCTYPE html>
<html lang="en">
<head>
    <meta charset="UTF-8">
    <title>Update Instance</title>
</head>
<body>
    <h1>Update Instance</h1>
    <form method="post">
        {% csrf_token %}
```

```
        <input type="text" name="name" value="{{ instance.name }}"><br>
        <textarea name="description">{{ instance.description }}</textarea><br>
        <input type="submit" value="Update">
    </form>
</body>
</html>
```

URLs Configuration

Lastly, configure the URLs to map the views:

```python
from django.urls import path
from myapp import views

urlpatterns = [
    path('', views.index, name='index'),
    path('create/', views.create, name='create'),
    path('update/<int:id>/', views.update, name='update'),
    path('delete/<int:id>/', views.delete, name='delete'),
]
```

With these configurations, you can now perform CRUD operations easily in your Django application. Django's built-in admin interface also provides a convenient way to perform these operations out of the box.

Chapter 5

Understanding URL Patterns and Mapping

Understanding URL patterns and mapping is crucial in Django development as it defines how URLs are mapped to views within your web application. In this guide, we'll delve into the concept of URL patterns and mapping in Django, complete with code examples for better comprehension.

URL Patterns in Django

URL patterns in Django are defined in the `urls.py` file of each Django app. They dictate how URLs are mapped to views, which are Python functions that handle HTTP requests and return HTTP responses.

Let's create a new Django app to demonstrate URL patterns:

```bash
python manage.py startapp myapp
```

Now, let's define some views and URL patterns within this app.

Defining Views

In the `views.py` file of your app, define some views:

```python
from django.http import HttpResponse

def home(request):
    return HttpResponse("Welcome to the homepage!")

def about(request):
    return HttpResponse("This is the about page.")
```

Mapping URLs to Views

Now, let's map URLs to these views in the `urls.py` file of the app.

```python
from django.urls import path
from . import views

urlpatterns = [
    path('', views.home, name='home'),
    path('about/', views.about, name='about'),
]
```

In this example:

- The empty string `''` corresponds to the root URL (e.g., `http://localhost:8000/`).

- `about/` corresponds to the `about` URL (e.g., `http://localhost:8000/about/`).

Including App URLs in Project URLs

To make these app-specific URLs accessible in the project, we need to include them in the project's `urls.py`.

In the project's `urls.py`, include the app's URL patterns:

```python
from django.contrib import admin
from django.urls import path, include

urlpatterns = [
    path('admin/', admin.site.urls),
    path('', include('myapp.urls')),
]
```

Now, when you run your Django project and navigate to `http://localhost:8000/`, it will route to the `home` view, and `http://localhost:8000/about/` will route to the `about` view.

Passing Parameters in URLs

URL patterns in Django support capturing parameters from the URL and passing them to views. Let's extend our example to demonstrate this:

```python
# myapp/views.py
def greet(request, name):
    return HttpResponse(f"Hello, {name}!")
```

```python
# myapp/urls.py
urlpatterns = [
    ...
    path('greet/<str:name>/', views.greet, name='greet'),
]
```

Now, if you navigate to `http://localhost:8000/greet/John/`, it will display "Hello, John!".

Regular Expressions in URL Patterns

Django URL patterns also support regular expressions for more complex URL matching. Let's create an example where we match numeric IDs:

```python
# myapp/views.py
def show_post(request, post_id):
    return HttpResponse(f"Showing post {post_id}")
```

```python
# myapp/urls.py
from django.urls import re_path

urlpatterns = [
    ...
    re_path(r'^post/(?P<post_id>\d+)/$', views.show_post, name='show_post'),
]
```

This pattern will match URLs like `http://localhost:8000/post/123/`, where `123` is the post ID.

Naming URL Patterns

Naming URL patterns allows you to reference them by name in templates or view functions. Let's name our existing URL patterns:

```python
# myapp/urls.py
urlpatterns = [
    ...
    path('', views.home, name='home'),
    path('about/', views.about, name='about'),
    path('greet/<str:name>/', views.greet, name='greet'),
    re_path(r'^post/(?P<post_id>\d+)/$', views.show_post, name='show_post'),
]
```

Now, you can refer to these URLs by their names, which makes your code more robust and maintainable.

Reverse URL Resolution

Django provides a `reverse` function to dynamically build URLs by their names. Let's see an example of how to use it in a view:

```python
```

```
from django.urls import reverse
from django.http import HttpResponseRedirect

def redirect_to_home(request):
    return HttpResponseRedirect(reverse('home'))
```

This view will redirect users to the homepage, regardless of the actual URL pattern defined for it.

URL Namespace

In larger projects with multiple apps, it's beneficial to organize URLs using namespaces to avoid naming conflicts. Let's demonstrate this with multiple apps:

```python
# myapp/urls.py
app_name = 'myapp'

urlpatterns = [
    ...
    path('', views.home, name='home'),
    path('about/', views.about, name='about'),
    ...
]
```

Now, in the project's `urls.py`, include these apps with namespaces:

```python
# project/urls.py
from django.urls import path, include

urlpatterns = [
    ...
    path('myapp/', include('myapp.urls', namespace='myapp')),
    path('otherapp/', include('otherapp.urls', namespace='otherapp')),
    ...
]
```

This way, you can refer to specific URLs using their namespaces, which helps in avoiding naming clashes.

Understanding URL patterns and mapping is fundamental in Django development as it dictates how URLs are routed to views. By defining URL patterns and mapping them to views, you can create a logical structure for your web application, making it easy to navigate and maintain. With Django's robust routing system, you can handle various URL configurations, including passing parameters, using regular expressions, and managing namespaces, ensuring flexibility and scalability in your projects.

Crafting Views: The Heart of User Interaction

Crafting views is a crucial aspect of Django development as views are responsible for handling user requests, processing data, and returning appropriate responses. In this guide, we'll explore the process of crafting views in Django, complete with code examples to illustrate various concepts.

Understanding Views in Django

In Django, views are Python functions or classes that receive HTTP requests and return HTTP responses. Views encapsulate the logic of your application and determine how data is presented to users.

Let's create a simple view to understand the basics:

```python
# views.py
from django.http import HttpResponse

def my_view(request):
    return HttpResponse("Hello, Django!")
```

In this example, `my_view` is a simple function-based view that returns a basic HTTP response.

Mapping URLs to Views

Once you've defined your views, you need to map them to specific URLs so that users can access them. This is done using URL patterns, as we discussed earlier. Here's how you can map the `my_view` to a URL:

```python
# urls.py
from django.urls import path
from . import views

urlpatterns = [
    path('hello/', views.my_view, name='hello'),
]
```

Now, when users navigate to `/hello/` on your website, they'll see the "Hello, Django!" message returned by the `my_view` function.

Passing Parameters to Views

Views often need to receive parameters from the URL or request body to perform specific tasks. Let's modify our view to accept a parameter:

```python
# views.py
def greet(request, name):
    return HttpResponse(f"Hello, {name}!")
```

```python
# urls.py
urlpatterns = [
    path('greet/<str:name>/', views.greet, name='greet'),
]
```

Now, when users navigate to `/greet/John/`, the view will return "Hello, John!".

Template Rendering

Views in Django often render HTML templates to generate dynamic content. Let's create a simple template and render it from a view:

```html
<!-- hello.html -->
```

```
<!DOCTYPE html>
<html lang="en">
<head>
   <meta charset="UTF-8">
   <title>Hello, Django!</title>
</head>
<body>
   <h1>Hello, Django!</h1>
</body>
</html>
```

```python
# views.py
from django.shortcuts import render

def hello_template(request):
    return render(request, 'hello.html')
```

```python
# urls.py
urlpatterns = [
    path('hello-template/', views.hello_template, name='hello_template'),
]
```

Now, when users navigate to `/hello-template/`, they'll see the HTML content defined in the `hello.html` template.

Handling Form Submissions

Views in Django are also responsible for handling form submissions and processing user input. Let's create a simple form and handle its submission in a view:

```html
<!-- form.html -->
<!DOCTYPE html>
<html lang="en">
<head>
    <meta charset="UTF-8">
    <title>Form Example</title>
</head>
<body>
    <form method="post">
        {% csrf_token %}
        <label for="name">Name:</label>
        <input type="text" id="name" name="name">
        <button type="submit">Submit</button>
    </form>
</body>
</html>
```

```python
# views.py
def handle_form(request):
    if request.method == 'POST':
        name = request.POST.get('name')
        return HttpResponse(f"Hello, {name}!")
    return render(request, 'form.html')
```

```python
# urls.py
urlpatterns = [
    path('form/', views.handle_form, name='form'),
]
```

Now, when users submit the form, the view will process the input and return a personalized greeting.

Class-Based Views

While function-based views are simple and straightforward, Django also provides class-based views (CBVs) for more complex scenarios. CBVs offer reusable components and built-in functionalities for common tasks. Let's convert our previous view to a class-based view:

```python
# views.py
from django.views import View

class GreetView(View):
    def get(self, request, *args, **kwargs):
        name = kwargs.get('name')
        return HttpResponse(f"Hello, {name}!")

    def post(self, request, *args, **kwargs):
        name = request.POST.get('name')
        return HttpResponse(f"Hello, {name}!")
```

```python
# urls.py
from .views import GreetView

urlpatterns = [
    path('greet-class-based/<str:name>/', GreetView.as_view(), name='greet_class_based'),
]
```

In this example, `GreetView` is a class-based view that handles both GET and POST requests.

Crafting views is at the heart of user interaction in Django applications. Views determine how data is presented to users, handle form submissions, process user input, and render HTML templates. Whether you choose function-based views or class-based views depends on the complexity of your application and your personal preference. By understanding the concepts discussed in this guide and experimenting with different view implementations, you'll be well-equipped to build dynamic and interactive web applications with Django.

Handling User Input and Form Processing

Handling user input and form processing is a crucial aspect of web development, allowing users to interact with web applications by submitting data through forms. In Django, handling user input and processing forms is streamlined and efficient. In this guide, we'll explore how to handle user input and process forms in Django, complete with code examples.

Creating a Simple Form

Let's start by creating a simple form in Django. Suppose we want to create a form for users to submit their feedback. First, we'll define the form in a new file named `forms.py` within our app:

```python
```

```python
# forms.py
from django import forms

class FeedbackForm(forms.Form):
    name = forms.CharField(label='Your Name', max_length=100)
    email = forms.EmailField(label='Your Email')
    message = forms.CharField(label='Your Message', widget=forms.Textarea)
```

In this form:

- We've created a `FeedbackForm` class that inherits from `forms.Form`.

- It contains three fields: `name`, `email`, and `message`.

- Each field is associated with an appropriate form field type (`CharField` and `EmailField`) and label.

Rendering the Form in a Template

Next, let's render this form in a template (`feedback_form.html`) using Django's template language:

```html
<!-- feedback_form.html -->
<!DOCTYPE html>
<html lang="en">
<head>
    <meta charset="UTF-8">
    <title>Feedback Form</title>
</head>
<body>
    <h1>Feedback Form</h1>
    <form method="post">
        {% csrf_token %}
        {{ form.as_p }}
        <button type="submit">Submit</button>
    </form>
</body>
</html>
```

In this template:

- We use `{{ form.as_p }}` to render the form fields as HTML paragraph elements.

- `{% csrf_token %}` is included to prevent Cross-Site Request Forgery (CSRF) attacks.

Handling Form Submission

Now, let's handle the form submission in a Django view. We'll create a view that renders the form initially and processes the form data when it's submitted:

```python
# views.py
from django.shortcuts import render
from .forms import FeedbackForm

def feedback_view(request):
    if request.method == 'POST':
        form = FeedbackForm(request.POST)
        if form.is_valid():
            # Process the form data
            name = form.cleaned_data['name']
            email = form.cleaned_data['email']
            message = form.cleaned_data['message']
            # Here, you can perform further processing such as saving to database, sending emails, etc.
            return render(request, 'success.html', {'name': name})
    else:
        form = FeedbackForm()
    return render(request, 'feedback_form.html', {'form': form})
```

In this view:

- We import the `FeedbackForm` class from `forms.py`.

- If the request method is POST, we create an instance of the form with the data submitted by the user (`request.POST`).

- We then validate the form using `form.is_valid()`. If the form is valid, we retrieve the cleaned data from the form and process it accordingly.

- If the form is not valid or if the request method is GET, we render the form initially.

Displaying Success Message

Finally, let's create a template to display a success message after the form is submitted successfully:

```html
<!-- success.html -->
<!DOCTYPE html>
<html lang="en">
<head>
```

```
    <meta charset="UTF-8">
    <title>Feedback Submitted</title>
</head>
<body>
    <h1>Thank You, {{ name }}!</h1>
    <p>Your feedback has been submitted successfully.</p>
</body>
</html>
```

Connecting URLs

To make the `feedback_view` accessible via a URL, we need to define a URL pattern:

```python
# urls.py
from django.urls import path
from . import views

urlpatterns = [
    path('feedback/', views.feedback_view, name='feedback'),
]
```

Handling user input and form processing is essential for building interactive web applications. In Django, this process is made straightforward with the help of Django's form handling capabilities. By defining forms, rendering them in templates, processing form submissions in views, and displaying appropriate responses, you can create robust and user-friendly forms in your Django applications. Experiment with different form field types, validation rules, and processing logic to tailor your forms to your specific requirements. With Django's powerful form handling features, you can build forms that meet the needs of your users and enhance the functionality of your web applications.

Chapter 6

Introduction to Django Templates (Jinja2)

Django templates, powered by the Jinja2 templating engine, are an essential component of building dynamic web applications with Django. They allow you to generate HTML dynamically by combining static HTML with template tags, template variables, and control structures. In this guide, we'll introduce you to Django templates and explore their features with code examples.

Understanding Django Templates

Django templates are text files that contain a mixture of static HTML and template tags. These tags provide control flow and logic for rendering dynamic content. Django uses the Jinja2 templating engine, which offers a powerful and flexible syntax for building templates.

Creating a Simple Template

Let's start by creating a simple Django template file. Create a new file named `index.html` in your app's `templates` directory:

```html
<!-- index.html -->
```

```html
<!DOCTYPE html>
<html lang="en">
<head>
    <meta charset="UTF-8">
    <title>Welcome to My Website</title>
</head>
<body>
    <h1>Welcome to My Website</h1>
    <p>Hello, {{ username }}!</p>
</body>
</html>
```

In this template:

- We've defined a basic HTML structure with a heading (`<h1>`) and a paragraph (`<p>`).

- The `{{ username }}` is a template variable that will be replaced with actual data when the template is rendered.

Rendering Templates in Views

To render this template in a view, we need to create a view function and return an HTTP response with the rendered template. Let's create a simple view:

```python
# views.py
from django.shortcuts import render

def index_view(request):
    username = "John"  # Assume we have retrieved the username from the database
    return render(request, 'index.html', {'username': username})
```

In this view:

- We import the `render` function from `django.shortcuts`.

- We define a view function `index_view` that takes a `request` object.

- We define a `username` variable (in this case, it's hardcoded, but you would typically retrieve it from a database or elsewhere).

- We call the `render` function, passing in the `request`, the name of the template file (`index.html`), and a dictionary containing template variables (`{'username': username}`).

Connecting URLs

To make the `index_view` accessible via a URL, we need to define a URL pattern:

```python
# urls.py
from django.urls import path
from . import views

urlpatterns = [
    path('', views.index_view, name='index'),
]
```

Template Inheritance

One of the powerful features of Django templates is template inheritance, which allows you to define a base template with common elements and extend it in child templates to override specific blocks. Let's create a base template (`base.html`) and a child template (`child.html`) to demonstrate this:

```html
<!-- base.html -->
<!DOCTYPE html>
<html lang="en">
```

```
<head>
    <meta charset="UTF-8">
    <title>{% block title %}My Website{% endblock %}</title>
</head>
<body>
    <header>
        <h1>My Website</h1>
    </header>
    <main>
        {% block content %}
        {% endblock %}
    </main>
    <footer>
        <p>&copy; 2024 My Website</p>
    </footer>
</body>
</html>
```

```html
<!-- child.html -->
{% extends 'base.html' %}

{% block title %}Child Page - My Website{% endblock %}

{% block content %}
```

```
<p>This is the content of the child page.</p>
{% endblock %}
```

In this example:

- The `base.html` template defines the basic structure of the website, including header, main content area, and footer.

- The `child.html` template extends `base.html` using `` `{% extends 'base.html' %}` `` and overrides the title and content blocks with specific content.

Template Tags and Filters

Django templates provide various built-in template tags and filters for performing common tasks such as looping over data, formatting dates, and applying conditional logic. Let's see some examples:

```html
<!-- Looping over a list -->
<ul>
    {% for item in items %}
    <li>{{ item }}</li>
    {% endfor %}
</ul>
```

```
<!-- Formatting a date -->
<p>{{ date_created | date:'F d, Y' }}</p>

<!-- Applying conditional logic -->
{% if user.is_authenticated %}
    <p>Welcome, {{ user.username }}!</p>
{% else %}
    <p>Please log in to continue.</p>
{% endif %}
```
```

Django templates, powered by the Jinja2 templating engine, provide a powerful and flexible way to generate HTML dynamically in Django applications. By combining static HTML with template tags, variables, control structures, and template inheritance, you can create dynamic and interactive web pages with ease. Experiment with different features of Django templates, such as template tags, filters, and template inheritance, to build robust and user-friendly web applications. With Django's templating engine, you can create dynamic content that meets the needs of your users and enhances the functionality of your web applications.
```

Using Variables, Filters, and Tags to Dynamically Generate Content

Using variables, filters, and tags in Django templates is essential for dynamically generating content and enhancing the functionality of web applications. These features allow you to manipulate data, apply formatting, and control the flow of your templates. In this guide, we'll explore how to use variables, filters, and tags effectively in Django templates, accompanied by code examples.

Using Variables in Templates

Variables in Django templates allow you to display dynamic content by inserting values passed from views. Let's start with a simple example:

```python
# views.py
from django.shortcuts import render

def index(request):
    context = {
        'username': 'John',
        'age': 30,
    }
    return render(request, 'index.html', context)
```

```

```html
<!-- index.html -->
<!DOCTYPE html>
<html lang="en">
<head>
  <meta charset="UTF-8">
  <title>Welcome</title>
</head>
<body>
  <h1>Welcome, {{ username }}</h1>
  <p>You are {{ age }} years old.</p>
</body>
</html>
```

In this example:

- In the view function, we define a dictionary `context` containing the `username` and `age` variables.

- We pass this dictionary as the third argument to the `render` function, making these variables available in the template.
```

- In the template, we use double curly braces `{{ ... }}` to output the values of the `username` and `age` variables.

Using Filters

Filters in Django templates allow you to modify the output of variables. Django provides a wide range of built-in filters for common tasks such as formatting dates, converting text to uppercase, and filtering lists. Let's see some examples:

```html
<!-- Formatting a date -->
<p>{{ my_date | date:"F d, Y" }}</p>

<!-- Converting text to uppercase -->
<p>{{ my_text | upper }}</p>

<!-- Truncating text -->
<p>{{ my_long_text | truncatewords:10 }}</p>

<!-- Joining a list -->
<p>{{ my_list | join:", " }}</p>
```

In these examples:

- We use the pipe `|` character to apply filters to variables.

- Filters accept arguments separated by colons `:` (e.g., `date` filter accepts a date format string).

- Filters can be chained together (e.g., `truncatewords:10` truncates the text to the first 10 words).

Using Tags

Tags in Django templates provide control flow and logic for rendering dynamic content. Let's explore some commonly used tags:

If Statement

```html
{% if user.is_authenticated %}
    <p>Welcome, {{ user.username }}!</p>
{% else %}
    <p>Please log in to continue.</p>
{% endif %}
```

In this example:

- We use the `{% if %}` and `{% else %}` tags to conditionally render content based on whether the user is authenticated.

- The `user.is_authenticated` variable is provided by Django's authentication system.

For Loop

```html
<ul>
    {% for item in items %}
        <li>{{ item }}</li>
    {% endfor %}
</ul>
```

In this example:

- We use the `{% for %}` and `{% endfor %}` tags to loop over a list of items.

- The `items` variable contains the list of items passed from the view.

Block Tag

```html
```

```
{% block content %}
  <h1>Welcome</h1>
  <p>This is the content of the page.</p>
{% endblock %}
```

In this example:

- We use the `{% block %}` and `{% endblock %}` tags to define a block of content that can be overridden in child templates.

- Child templates can extend this template and override specific blocks as needed.

Using Variables, Filters, and Tags Together

Let's combine variables, filters, and tags to create a more complex example:

```python
# views.py
from django.shortcuts import render

def blog(request):
    posts = [
        {'title': 'Post 1', 'content': 'Content of post 1', 'date': '2024-06-01'},
```

```
        {'title': 'Post 2', 'content': 'Content of post 2', 'date':
'2024-06-02'},
        {'title': 'Post 3', 'content': 'Content of post 3', 'date':
'2024-06-03'},
    ]
    return render(request, 'blog.html', {'posts': posts})
```

```html
<!-- blog.html -->
<!DOCTYPE html>
<html lang="en">
<head>
    <meta charset="UTF-8">
    <title>Blog</title>
</head>
<body>
    <h1>Blog</h1>
    <ul>
        {% for post in posts %}
            <li>
                <h2>{{ post.title }}</h2>
                <p>{{ post.content | truncatewords:10 }}</p>
                <p>Published on {{ post.date | date:"F d, Y" }}</p>
            </li>
        {% endfor %}
    </ul>
```

```
</body>
</html>
```

In this example:

- We define a list of blog posts in the view function and pass it to the template.

- In the template, we use a `{% for %}` loop to iterate over each post in the list.

- We use filters to truncate the content of each post and format the publication date.

Using variables, filters, and tags in Django templates allows you to generate dynamic and interactive content for your web applications. By combining these features effectively, you can create templates that adapt to different data and display information in a user-friendly manner. Experiment with different filters, control structures, and template logic to customize the appearance and behavior of your templates according to your specific requirements. With Django's powerful templating engine, you can build dynamic and engaging web applications that meet the needs of your users.

Creating Beautiful and Functional User Interfaces

Creating beautiful and functional user interfaces is essential for providing a positive user experience in web applications. In Django full stack development, you can achieve this by combining Django's powerful backend capabilities with modern front-end technologies like HTML, CSS, and JavaScript. In this guide, we'll explore how to create beautiful and functional user interfaces in Django, complete with code examples and best practices.

Designing User Interfaces with HTML and CSS

HTML and CSS are the backbone of web design, allowing you to structure and style web pages. Let's start by creating a simple HTML template for a user interface:

```html
<!-- base.html -->
<!DOCTYPE html>
<html lang="en">
<head>
    <meta charset="UTF-8">
    <title>{% block title %}My Website{% endblock %}</title>
    <link rel="stylesheet" href="{% static 'css/styles.css' %}">
```

```
</head>
<body>
  <header>
    <h1>My Website</h1>
    <nav>
      <ul>
        <li><a href="{% url 'home' %}">Home</a></li>
        <li><a href="{% url 'about' %}">About</a></li>
        <li><a href="{% url 'contact' %}">Contact</a></li>
      </ul>
    </nav>
  </header>

  <main>
    {% block content %}
    {% endblock %}
  </main>

  <footer>
    <p>&copy; 2024 My Website</p>
  </footer>
</body>
</html>
```

In this template:

- We define a base HTML structure with header, main content area, and footer.

- We use template tags to dynamically generate URLs for navigation links.

- We include a link to an external stylesheet (`styles.css`) for styling.

Now, let's create a CSS file (`styles.css`) to add some basic styling:

```css
/* styles.css */
body {
    font-family: Arial, sans-serif;
    margin: 0;
    padding: 0;
}

header {
    background-color: #333;
    color: #fff;
    padding: 20px;
}
```

```css
nav ul {
    list-style-type: none;
    margin: 0;
    padding: 0;
}

nav ul li {
    display: inline;
    margin-right: 20px;
}

nav ul li a {
    color: #fff;
    text-decoration: none;
}

main {
    padding: 20px;
}

footer {
    background-color: #333;
    color: #fff;
    padding: 10px 20px;
    position: fixed;
    bottom: 0;
    width: 100%;
    text-align: center;
```

```
}
```

In this CSS file:

- We define styles for the body, header, navigation, main content area, and footer.

- We use basic styling properties like background color, font family, padding, and margins to improve the appearance of the user interface.

Enhancing User Interface with JavaScript

JavaScript allows you to add interactivity and dynamic behavior to your web pages. Let's add some JavaScript to our user interface to enhance its functionality:

```html
<!-- base.html -->
<!DOCTYPE html>
<html lang="en">
<head>
    <meta charset="UTF-8">
    <title>{% block title %}My Website{% endblock %}</title>
    <link rel="stylesheet" href="{% static 'css/styles.css' %}">
```

```
    <script src="{% static 'js/main.js' %}" defer></script>
</head>
<body>
    <!-- Header and Navigation -->

    <main>
        {% block content %}
        {% endblock %}
    </main>

    <!-- Footer -->

</body>
</html>
```

In this template:

- We include a link to an external JavaScript file (`main.js`) with the `defer` attribute to ensure it's loaded after the HTML content.

- We'll add JavaScript code to `main.js` to enhance the user interface.

Let's add some JavaScript code to `main.js` to create a simple interactive feature:

```javascript
// main.js
document.addEventListener('DOMContentLoaded', function() {
  const button = document.querySelector('#click-me');
  button.addEventListener('click', function() {
    alert('Button clicked!');
  });
});
```

In this JavaScript code:

- We use the `DOMContentLoaded` event to ensure the DOM is fully loaded before executing JavaScript.

- We select the button element with the ID `click-me` and attach a click event listener to it.

- When the button is clicked, an alert dialog will be displayed with the message "Button clicked!".

Integrating Frontend Frameworks

You can further enhance your user interface by integrating frontend frameworks like Bootstrap or Materialize CSS. These frameworks provide pre-designed components and stylesheets to create modern and responsive user interfaces quickly.

Let's integrate Bootstrap into our Django project:

1. Install Bootstrap using a package manager like npm:

```bash
npm install bootstrap
```

2. Include Bootstrap's CSS and JavaScript files in your template:

```html
<!-- base.html -->
<!DOCTYPE html>
<html lang="en">
<head>
    <meta charset="UTF-8">
    <title>{% block title %}My Website{% endblock %}</title>
    <link rel="stylesheet" href="{% static 'node_modules/bootstrap/dist/css/bootstrap.min.css' %}">
    <script src="{% static 'node_modules/bootstrap/dist/js/bootstrap.min.js' %}" defer></script>
```

```
</head>
<body>
  <!-- Header and Navigation -->

  <main>
    {% block content %}
    {% endblock %}
  </main>

  <!-- Footer -->

</body>
</html>
'''
```

Now, you can use Bootstrap classes and components to style your HTML elements and create a modern and responsive user interface.

Creating beautiful and functional user interfaces in Django involves a combination of HTML, CSS, JavaScript, and frontend frameworks. By designing well-structured HTML templates, applying CSS for styling, adding JavaScript for interactivity, and integrating frontend frameworks for modern design elements, you can create engaging and user-friendly web applications. Experiment with different design patterns, layout techniques, and frontend technologies to tailor your user interface to the specific needs of your application and audience. With Django's powerful backend capabilities and flexible frontend options, you can create web applications that not only look great but also provide a seamless and intuitive user experience.

Chapter 7

Unveiling the Front-End: HTML, CSS, and JavaScript

Building the Foundation with HTML Structure

Building the foundation with HTML structure is crucial for creating well-organized and semantically meaningful web pages in Django full stack development. HTML provides the structure and layout for your web pages, while Django handles the backend logic and data management. In this guide, we'll explore how to build the foundation of your Django project with HTML structure, complete with code examples and best practices.

Understanding HTML Structure

HTML (Hypertext Markup Language) is the standard markup language for creating web pages. It defines the structure and content of a web page using elements such as headings, paragraphs, lists, and links. Let's start by creating a basic HTML structure for a Django project:

```html
<!DOCTYPE html>
<html lang="en">
```

```html
<head>
    <meta charset="UTF-8">
    <meta name="viewport" content="width=device-width, initial-scale=1.0">
    <title>My Django Project</title>
</head>
<body>

    <!-- Header -->
    <header>
        <h1>Welcome to My Django Project</h1>
        <nav>
            <ul>
                <li><a href="/">Home</a></li>
                <li><a href="/about">About</a></li>
                <li><a href="/contact">Contact</a></li>
            </ul>
        </nav>
    </header>

    <!-- Main Content -->
    <main>
        {% block content %}
        {% endblock %}
    </main>

    <!-- Footer -->
    <footer>
```

```
            <p>&copy; 2024 My Django Project</p>
        </footer>

</body>
</html>
```

In this HTML structure:

- We start with the `<!DOCTYPE html>` declaration, which specifies the document type and version of HTML being used.

- The `<html>` element represents the root of the HTML document and specifies the language of the document.

- The `<head>` element contains metadata about the document, such as character encoding, viewport settings, and title.

- Inside the `<body>` element, we have the main sections of the web page: header, main content, and footer.

- We use semantic HTML elements like `<header>`, `<nav>`, `<main>`, and `<footer>` to provide meaning and structure to the content.

- We use Django template tags `{% block content %}` and `{% endblock %}` to define a block of content that can be overridden in child templates.

Organizing Content with Semantic HTML Elements

Semantic HTML elements provide meaning and context to the content of a web page, making it easier for search engines, screen readers, and developers to understand the structure of the document. Let's explore some common semantic HTML elements and how they can be used in a Django project:

- `<header>`: Represents the introductory content or navigation links at the top of a web page.

- `<nav>`: Defines a section of navigation links.

- `<main>`: Contains the main content of the web page.

- `<section>`: Represents a thematic grouping of content, typically with a heading.

- `<article>`: Represents a self-contained piece of content, such as a blog post or news article.

- `<aside>`: Represents content that is tangentially related to the main content, such as a sidebar or related links.

- `<footer>`: Contains footer information, such as copyright notices or contact information.

By using semantic HTML elements, you can create well-structured and accessible web pages that are easier to maintain and understand.

Integrating Django Template Language

In a Django project, you can use the Django template language to generate dynamic content and include reusable components in your HTML templates. Let's see how you can integrate Django template tags and variables into your HTML structure:

```html
<!-- base.html -->
<!DOCTYPE html>
<html lang="en">
<head>
    <meta charset="UTF-8">
    <meta name="viewport" content="width=device-width, initial-scale=1.0">
```

```html
    <title>{% block title %}My Django Project{% endblock %}</title>
</head>
<body>

    <!-- Header -->
    <header>
        <h1>Welcome to My Django Project</h1>
        <nav>
            <ul>
                <li><a href="{% url 'home' %}">Home</a></li>
                <li><a href="{% url 'about' %}">About</a></li>
                <li><a href="{% url 'contact' %}">Contact</a></li>
            </ul>
        </nav>
    </header>

    <!-- Main Content -->
    <main>
       {% block content %}
       {% endblock %}
    </main>

    <!-- Footer -->
    <footer>
```

```
        <p>&copy; 2024 My Django Project</p>
    </footer>

</body>
</html>
```

In this HTML structure:

- We use Django template tags `{% block title %}` and `{% endblock %}` to define a block of content for the page title that can be overridden in child templates.

- We use the `{% url %}` template tag to generate URLs for navigation links dynamically.

Creating Child Templates

Now, let's create a child template that extends the base template and overrides the content block:

```html
<!-- home.html -->
{% extends 'base.html' %}

{% block title %}Home - My Django Project{% endblock %}
```

```
{% block content %}
   <section>
      <h2>Home Page</h2>
      <p>Welcome to the home page of My Django Project.</p>
   </section>
{% endblock %}
```

In this child template:

- We use the `{% extends %}` template tag to inherit from the base template (`base.html`).

- We override the `{% block title %}` block with a specific title for the home page.

- We override the `{% block content %}` block with the content specific to the home page.

Building the foundation with HTML structure is essential for creating well-organized and semantically meaningful web pages in Django full stack development. By using semantic HTML elements, integrating Django template language, and organizing content into reusable templates, you can create a solid foundation for your Django project. Experiment with different HTML elements, Django template tags, and template inheritance to create web pages that are both functional and user-friendly. With a well-structured HTML foundation, you can efficiently build and maintain complex web applications in Django.

Styling Websites with CSS: Defining Visual Appeal

Styling websites with CSS is crucial for defining the visual appeal and user experience of web pages in Django full stack development. CSS (Cascading Style Sheets) allows you to control the layout, colors, fonts, and other visual aspects of your web pages. In this guide, we'll explore how to style websites with CSS in Django, accompanied by code examples and best practices.

Understanding CSS Basics

CSS defines the presentation of HTML elements on a web page. It works by selecting HTML elements and applying styles to them. Let's start with some basic CSS syntax:

```css
/* styles.css */

/* Selectors */
body {
```

```
    font-family: Arial, sans-serif;
}

h1 {
   color: #333;
}

p {
   font-size: 16px;
   line-height: 1.5;
}
```

In this CSS code:

- We use selectors to target HTML elements (`body`, `h1`, `p`) and apply styles to them.

- We use property-value pairs to define specific styles (e.g., `font-family`, `color`, `font-size`, `line-height`).

Integrating CSS into Django Templates

To apply CSS styles to your Django project, you can create a separate CSS file and link it to your HTML templates. Let's see how you can integrate CSS into your Django project:

1. Create a CSS file (`styles.css`) in your static files directory (`static/css`):

```css
/* static/css/styles.css */
body {
    font-family: Arial, sans-serif;
}

h1 {
    color: #333;
}

p {
    font-size: 16px;
    line-height: 1.5;
}
```

2. Link the CSS file in your HTML template (`base.html`):

```html
<!-- base.html -->
<!DOCTYPE html>
<html lang="en">
<head>
```

```
    <meta charset="UTF-8">
    <meta name="viewport" content="width=device-width, initial-scale=1.0">
    <title>{% block title %}My Django Project{% endblock %}</title>
    <link rel="stylesheet" href="{% static 'css/styles.css' %}">
</head>
<body>

    <!-- Header, Main Content, Footer -->

</body>
</html>
```

In this HTML code:

- We use the `{% static %}` template tag to generate the URL for the CSS file dynamically.

- We link the CSS file using the `<link>` element in the `<head>` section of the HTML document.

Applying Styles to HTML Elements

Now that we've linked our CSS file to our HTML templates, let's explore how to apply styles to specific HTML elements:

```css
/* styles.css */

/* Selectors */
header {
    background-color: #333;
    color: #fff;
    padding: 20px;
}

nav ul {
    list-style-type: none;
    margin: 0;
    padding: 0;
}

nav ul li {
    display: inline;
    margin-right: 20px;
}

nav ul li a {
    color: #fff;
    text-decoration: none;
```

```
}

main {
  padding: 20px;
}

footer {
  background-color: #333;
  color: #fff;
  padding: 10px 20px;
  position: fixed;
  bottom: 0;
  width: 100%;
  text-align: center;
}
```

In this CSS code:

- We apply styles to specific HTML elements such as `header`, `nav`, `ul`, `li`, `a`, `main`, and `footer`.

- We use various CSS properties like `background-color`, `color`, `padding`, `display`, `margin`, `position`, and `text-align` to define the appearance and layout of these elements.

Using CSS Frameworks

CSS frameworks like Bootstrap, Foundation, or Bulma provide pre-designed components and stylesheets to create modern and responsive web interfaces quickly. Let's integrate Bootstrap into our Django project:

1. Install Bootstrap using a package manager like npm:

```bash
npm install bootstrap
```

2. Link Bootstrap's CSS and JavaScript files in your HTML template (`base.html`):

```html
<!-- base.html -->
<!DOCTYPE html>
<html lang="en">
<head>
    <meta charset="UTF-8">
    <meta name="viewport" content="width=device-width, initial-scale=1.0">
    <title>{% block title %}My Django Project{% endblock %}</title>
```

```
    <link rel="stylesheet" href="{% static
'node_modules/bootstrap/dist/css/bootstrap.min.css'
%}">
    <script src="{% static
'node_modules/bootstrap/dist/js/bootstrap.min.js' %}"
defer></script>
</head>
<body>

    <!-- Header, Main Content, Footer -->

</body>
</html>
```

Now, you can use Bootstrap classes and components to style your HTML elements and create a modern and responsive user interface.

Styling websites with CSS is essential for defining the visual appeal and user experience of web pages in Django full stack development. By using CSS to control the layout, colors, fonts, and other visual aspects of your web pages, you can create engaging and user-friendly interfaces for your Django projects. Experiment with different CSS properties, selectors, and frameworks to customize the appearance and behavior of your web pages according to your specific requirements. With

CSS, you can enhance the aesthetics and usability of your Django applications, making them more attractive and functional for your users.

Adding Interactivity with JavaScript: Making Websites Dynamic

Adding interactivity with JavaScript is essential for making websites dynamic and engaging in Django full stack development. JavaScript allows you to add functionality such as form validation, DOM manipulation, event handling, and asynchronous communication to your web pages. In this guide, we'll explore how to add interactivity with JavaScript in Django, complete with code examples and best practices.

Understanding JavaScript Basics

JavaScript is a scripting language that runs in the browser and allows you to create interactive web pages. It provides functionality for handling events, manipulating the DOM (Document Object Model), making HTTP requests, and more. Let's start with some basic JavaScript syntax:

```javascript
// main.js

// Event Listener
```

```
document.addEventListener('DOMContentLoaded', 
function() {
    // DOM manipulation
    const heading = document.querySelector('h1');
    heading.textContent = 'Hello, JavaScript!';

    // Event handling
    const button = document.querySelector('#my-button');
    button.addEventListener('click', function() {
        alert('Button clicked!');
    });
```

In this JavaScript code:

- We use the `addEventListener()` method to attach an event listener to the `DOMContentLoaded` event, which fires when the DOM is fully loaded.

- Inside the event listener function, we manipulate the DOM by selecting an HTML element (`<h1>`) and changing its text content.

- We also handle events by selecting a button element (`<button>`) and adding a click event listener to it. When the button is clicked, an alert dialog will be displayed with the message "Button clicked!".

Integrating JavaScript into Django Templates

To add JavaScript functionality to your Django project, you can create a separate JavaScript file and link it to your HTML templates. Let's see how you can integrate JavaScript into your Django project:

1. Create a JavaScript file (`main.js`) in your static files directory (`static/js`):

```javascript
// static/js/main.js

document.addEventListener('DOMContentLoaded', function() {
    // Your JavaScript code here
});
```

2. Link the JavaScript file in your HTML template (`base.html`):

```html
<!-- base.html -->
<!DOCTYPE html>
```

```
<html lang="en">
<head>
  <meta charset="UTF-8">
  <meta name="viewport" content="width=device-width, initial-scale=1.0">
  <title>{% block title %}My Django Project{% endblock %}</title>
</head>
<body>

  <!-- Header, Main Content, Footer -->

  <script src="{% static 'js/main.js' %}" defer></script>
</body>
</html>
```

In this HTML code:

- We use the `{% static %}` template tag to generate the URL for the JavaScript file dynamically.

- We link the JavaScript file using the `<script>` element at the end of the `<body>` section of the HTML document, with the `defer` attribute to ensure it's executed after the HTML content is parsed.

Adding Interactivity to Django Templates

Now, let's explore some common scenarios where you can add interactivity with JavaScript to your Django templates:

Form Validation

```javascript
// main.js

document.addEventListener('DOMContentLoaded', function() {
    const form = document.querySelector('#my-form');
    const emailInput = document.querySelector('#email');

    form.addEventListener('submit', function(event) {
        if (!emailInput.value.includes('@')) {
            event.preventDefault();
            alert('Please enter a valid email address.');
        }
    });
});
```

In this JavaScript code:

- We select the form element (`<form>`) and the email input field (`<input type="email">`) using the `querySelector()` method.

- We attach a submit event listener to the form.

- Inside the event listener function, we check if the email input value contains the '@' symbol. If not, we prevent the form from submitting and display an alert message.

Dynamic Content Loading

```javascript
// main.js

document.addEventListener('DOMContentLoaded', function() {
    const loadButton = document.querySelector('#load-button');
    const contentContainer = document.querySelector('#content-container');

    loadButton.addEventListener('click', function() {
        fetch('/api/data')
            .then(response => response.json())
            .then(data => {
                contentContainer.textContent = data.message;
```

```
        })
        .catch(error => {
            console.error('Error:', error);
    });
```

In this JavaScript code:

- We select a button element (`<button>`) and a container element (`<div>`) where we want to display dynamic content.

- We attach a click event listener to the button.

- Inside the event listener function, we use the `fetch()` function to make an HTTP request to a backend API endpoint (`/api/data`).

- We handle the response by converting it to JSON and updating the content of the container element with the received data.

Adding interactivity with JavaScript is essential for making websites dynamic and engaging in Django full stack development. By using JavaScript to handle events, manipulate the DOM, make HTTP requests, and more, you can create interactive user experiences that enhance the functionality and usability of your Django applications. Experiment with different JavaScript features and techniques to add interactivity to your Django templates according to your specific requirements. With JavaScript, you can make your Django projects more interactive, responsive, and user-friendly, ultimately improving the overall user experience.

Integrating Front-End Technologies with Django Templates

Integrating front-end technologies with Django templates is essential for creating modern and responsive web applications in Django full stack development. Front-end technologies such as HTML, CSS, JavaScript, and frontend frameworks like Bootstrap or Vue.js complement Django's backend capabilities, allowing you to build dynamic and interactive user interfaces. In this guide, we'll explore how to integrate front-end technologies with Django templates, complete with code examples and best practices.

Using HTML Templates in Django

Django uses a templating engine that allows you to dynamically generate HTML content using Python code. Let's start with a simple example of a Django template:

```html
```

```html
<!-- template.html -->
<!DOCTYPE html>
<html lang="en">
<head>
    <meta charset="UTF-8">
    <meta name="viewport" content="width=device-width, initial-scale=1.0">
    <title>{% block title %}My Website{% endblock %}</title>
</head>
<body>
    <h1>Welcome, {{ username }}</h1>
    <p>You are {{ age }} years old.</p>
</body>
</html>
```

In this Django template:

- We use template tags `{% block %}` and `{% endblock %}` to define a block of content that can be overridden in child templates.

- We use double curly braces `{{ ... }}` to output the values of variables passed from the view.

Styling Django Templates with CSS

You can apply styles to Django templates using CSS (Cascading Style Sheets) to improve their appearance and layout. Let's see how to integrate CSS into a Django template:

```css
/* styles.css */
body {
    font-family: Arial, sans-serif;
    background-color: #f0f0f0;
}

h1 {
    color: #333;
}

p {
    color: #666;
}
```

In this CSS file:

- We define styles for the body, headings, and paragraphs to change their font family and colors.

- We use a separate CSS file (`styles.css`) to keep the styles organized and reusable.

Adding Interactivity with JavaScript

JavaScript allows you to add interactivity and dynamic behavior to Django templates. Let's add a simple JavaScript function to the template:

```javascript
// main.js
function greetUser() {
    const username = document.querySelector('#username').textContent;
    alert('Hello, ' + username + '!');
}
```

```html
<!-- template.html -->
<!DOCTYPE html>
<html lang="en">
<head>
    <meta charset="UTF-8">
    <meta name="viewport" content="width=device-width, initial-scale=1.0">
    <title>{% block title %}My Website{% endblock %}</title>
    <script src="{% static 'js/main.js' %}"></script>
</head>
```

```
<body>
    <h1 id="username">John</h1>
    <button onclick="greetUser()">Greet</button>
</body>
</html>
```

In this example:

- We create a JavaScript function `greetUser()` that retrieves the username from an HTML element with the ID `username` and displays an alert message.

- We include the JavaScript file (`main.js`) in the HTML template and call the `greetUser()` function when a button is clicked.

Integrating Frontend Frameworks

You can enhance your Django templates by integrating frontend frameworks like Bootstrap, Foundation, or Vue.js. Let's integrate Bootstrap into a Django template:

1. Install Bootstrap using a package manager like npm:

```bash
npm install bootstrap
```

```

2. Include Bootstrap's CSS and JavaScript files in the Django template:

```html
<!-- template.html -->
<!DOCTYPE html>
<html lang="en">
<head>
    <meta charset="UTF-8">
    <meta name="viewport" content="width=device-width, initial-scale=1.0">
    <title>{% block title %}My Website{% endblock %}</title>
    <link rel="stylesheet" href="{% static 'node_modules/bootstrap/dist/css/bootstrap.min.css' %}">
    <script src="{% static 'node_modules/bootstrap/dist/js/bootstrap.min.js' %}"></script>
</head>
<body>
    <!-- Bootstrap components -->
    <div class="container">
        <div class="jumbotron">
            <h1 class="display-4">Welcome</h1>

```
        <p class="lead">This is a Bootstrap-themed
Django template.</p>
        <hr class="my-4">
        <p>It uses Bootstrap components to enhance the
design and layout.</p>
      </div>
   </div>
</body>
</html>
```

In this example:

- We link Bootstrap's CSS and JavaScript files in the HTML template to apply Bootstrap styles and functionality.

- We use Bootstrap components such as `container`, `jumbotron`, `display-4`, `lead`, and `my-4` classes to style the content and layout.

Integrating front-end technologies with Django templates allows you to create modern and responsive web applications with rich user interfaces. By using HTML templates, CSS for styling, JavaScript for interactivity, and frontend frameworks like Bootstrap, you can build dynamic and engaging user experiences for your Django projects. Experiment with different front-end technologies and techniques to customize the appearance and behavior of your Django templates according to your specific requirements. With the flexibility and power of Django's templating engine, you can create web applications that are both visually appealing and highly functional.

Chapter 8

Implementing User Registration, Login, and Logout Functionality

Implementing user registration, login, and logout functionality is essential for building secure and user-friendly web applications in Django full stack development. Django provides built-in authentication and authorization mechanisms that make it easy to implement these features. In this guide, we'll walk through the process of implementing user registration, login, and logout functionality in a Django project, complete with code examples and best practices.

Setting Up Django Authentication

Before implementing user registration, login, and logout functionality, make sure to enable Django's authentication system by adding ``django.contrib.auth`` to the `INSTALLED_APPS` setting in your Django project's `settings.py` file:

```python
# settings.py

INSTALLED_APPS = [
    ...
```

```
    'django.contrib.auth',
    ...
]
```

User Registration

To allow users to register on your website, you need to create a registration form and view. Let's start by creating a registration form using Django's built-in `UserCreationForm`:

```python
# forms.py
from django import forms
from django.contrib.auth.forms import UserCreationForm
from django.contrib.auth.models import User

class RegistrationForm(UserCreationForm):
    email = forms.EmailField(required=True)

    class Meta:
        model = User
        fields = ('username', 'email', 'password1', 'password2')
```

In this form:

- We inherit from `UserCreationForm` provided by Django.

- We add an email field to the form.

Next, let's create a view to handle the registration process:

```python
# views.py
from django.shortcuts import render, redirect
from .forms import RegistrationForm

def register(request):
    if request.method == 'POST':
        form = RegistrationForm(request.POST)
        if form.is_valid():
            form.save()
            return redirect('login')
    else:
        form = RegistrationForm()
    return render(request, 'registration/register.html', {'form': form})
```

In this view:

- We handle both GET and POST requests.

- If the form is valid, we save the user and redirect them to the login page.

- If the form is not valid or the request is not POST, we render the registration form template with the form.

Finally, create a registration form template (`register.html`) to render the registration form:

```html
<!-- register.html -->
<!DOCTYPE html>
<html lang="en">
<head>
    <meta charset="UTF-8">
    <meta name="viewport" content="width=device-width, initial-scale=1.0">
    <title>User Registration</title>
</head>
<body>
    <h1>User Registration</h1>
    <form method="post">
        {% csrf_token %}
        {{ form.as_p }}
```

```
        <button type="submit">Register</button>
    </form>
</body>
</html>
```

User Login

After registering, users should be able to log in to access restricted content. Django provides a built-in login form and view for this purpose:

```python
# views.py
from django.contrib.auth.forms import AuthenticationForm
from django.contrib.auth import login

def user_login(request):
    if request.method == 'POST':
        form = AuthenticationForm(data=request.POST)
        if form.is_valid():
            user = form.get_user()
            login(request, user)
            return redirect('home')
    else:
        form = AuthenticationForm()
```

```
    return render(request, 'registration/login.html', {'form': form})
```

In this view:

- We use Django's `AuthenticationForm` to handle user authentication.

- If the form is valid, we log in the user and redirect them to the home page.

- If the form is not valid or the request is not POST, we render the login form template with the form.

Create a login form template (`login.html`) to render the login form:

```html
<!-- login.html -->
<!DOCTYPE html>
<html lang="en">
<head>
    <meta charset="UTF-8">
    <meta name="viewport" content="width=device-width, initial-scale=1.0">
    <title>User Login</title>
```

```
</head>
<body>
  <h1>User Login</h1>
  <form method="post">
    {% csrf_token %}
    {{ form.as_p }}
    <button type="submit">Login</button>
  </form>
</body>
</html>
```

User Logout

Finally, users should be able to log out of the website. Django provides a built-in `logout` view for this purpose:

```python
# views.py
from django.contrib.auth import logout

def user_logout(request):
    logout(request)
    return redirect('home')
```

In this view:

- We simply call Django's `logout` function to log out the user.

- We then redirect the user to the home page.

URLs Configuration

Don't forget to configure the URLs for the registration, login, and logout views in your Django project's `urls.py` file:

```python
# urls.py
from django.urls import path
from . import views

urlpatterns = [
    path('register/', views.register, name='register'),
    path('login/', views.user_login, name='login'),
    path('logout/', views.user_logout, name='logout'),
]
```

Implementing user registration, login, and logout functionality is crucial for building secure and user-friendly web applications in Django. By following the steps outlined in this guide and using Django's built-in authentication system, you can easily add these features to your Django project. Remember to test your registration, login, and logout workflows thoroughly to ensure a smooth user experience. With Django's authentication system, you can create powerful web applications that meet the needs of your users while maintaining security and scalability.

Managing User Permissions and Access Control

Managing user permissions and access control is essential for ensuring the security and integrity of your Django web application. Django provides a robust authentication and authorization system that allows you to define user permissions and control access to different parts of your application. In this guide, we'll explore how to manage user permissions and access control in Django, complete with code examples and best practices.

Understanding User Permissions in Django

Django's permission system allows you to define specific actions that users can perform within your application. Permissions are associated with models and are used to control access to certain views, actions, or resources. Django provides several built-in permissions, such as `add`, `change`, and `delete`, which correspond to

CRUD operations (Create, Read, Update, Delete). Let's see how to define and assign permissions in Django:

1. Define Permissions in Models

```python
# models.py
from django.db import models
from django.contrib.auth.models import User

class Post(models.Model):
    title = models.CharField(max_length=100)
    content = models.TextField()
    author = models.ForeignKey(User, on_delete=models.CASCADE)

    class Meta:
        permissions = [
            ('can_view_post', 'Can view post'),
            ('can_edit_post', 'Can edit post'),
            ('can_delete_post', 'Can delete post'),
        ]
```

In this model:

- We define a `Post` model with fields for title, content, and author.

- We define custom permissions (`can_view_post`, `can_edit_post`, `can_delete_post`) associated with the `Post` model.

2. Assign Permissions to Users

```python
# views.py
from django.contrib.auth.models import Permission

def assign_permissions(request):
    user = request.user
    post_permissions = Permission.objects.filter(codename__in=['can_view_post', 'can_edit_post'])
    user.user_permissions.set(post_permissions)
```

In this view:

- We retrieve the current user (`request.user`).

- We filter the permissions we want to assign (`can_view_post`, `can_edit_post`).

- We assign the filtered permissions to the user using the `user_permissions.set()` method.

Checking User Permissions in Views

Once permissions are assigned to users, you can check if a user has a specific permission in your views to control access to certain functionalities. Let's see how to check user permissions in a view:

```python
# views.py
from django.shortcuts import render, get_object_or_404
from django.contrib.auth.decorators import permission_required
from .models import Post

@permission_required('blog.can_edit_post')
def edit_post(request, post_id):
    post = get_object_or_404(Post, pk=post_id)
    # Edit post logic...
```

In this view:

- We use the `@permission_required` decorator to require the `can_edit_post` permission.

- Only users who have the `can_edit_post` permission will be able to access the `edit_post` view.

Displaying Permissions in Templates

You can also display user permissions in your templates to provide users with information about their access rights. Let's see how to display user permissions in a template:

```html
<!-- permissions.html -->
<!DOCTYPE html>
<html lang="en">
<head>
    <meta charset="UTF-8">
    <meta name="viewport" content="width=device-width, initial-scale=1.0">
    <title>User Permissions</title>
</head>
<body>
    <h1>User Permissions</h1>
    <ul>
        {% for permission in user.get_all_permissions %}
            <li>{{ permission }}</li>
        {% endfor %}
    </ul>
```

```
</body>
</html>
```

In this template:

- We use the `get_all_permissions` method to retrieve all permissions associated with the current user.

- We iterate over the permissions using a for loop and display them in a list.

Managing user permissions and access control is crucial for ensuring the security and integrity of your Django web application. By using Django's built-in permission system, you can define specific actions that users can perform and control access to different parts of your application. Follow the steps outlined in this guide to define permissions in your models, assign permissions to users, check permissions in your views, and display permissions in your templates. With Django's powerful permission system, you can create secure and scalable web applications that meet the needs of your users while maintaining data integrity and confidentiality.

Securing Your Django Application

Securing your Django application is crucial to protect sensitive data, prevent unauthorized access, and ensure the integrity of your application. Django provides various security features and best practices to help you build secure web applications. In this guide, we'll explore how to secure your Django application, covering authentication, authorization, protection against common security threats, and other best practices.

Authentication and Authorization

1. User Authentication

Django provides a robust authentication system out of the box, allowing users to securely log in and manage their accounts. Use Django's built-in authentication views and forms to handle user authentication:

```python
# urls.py
from django.contrib.auth import views as auth_views

urlpatterns = [
    path('login/', auth_views.LoginView.as_view(), name='login'),
```

```
    path('logout/', auth_views.LogoutView.as_view(), name='logout'),
]
```

```html
<!-- login.html -->
<form method="post">
    {% csrf_token %}
    {{ form.as_p }}
    <button type="submit">Login</button>
</form>
```

2. User Authorization

Control access to different parts of your application by defining permissions and using Django's built-in authorization system. Use decorators or mixins to restrict access to views:

```python
# views.py
from django.contrib.auth.decorators import login_required

@login_required
def my_view(request):
```

```
# View logic...
```

Protection Against Common Security Threats

1. Cross-Site Request Forgery (CSRF) Protection

Django provides CSRF protection by default. Ensure that the `{% csrf_token %}` template tag is included in all forms to prevent CSRF attacks:

```html
<form method="post">
    {% csrf_token %}
    <!-- Form fields -->
</form>
```

2. Cross-Site Scripting (XSS) Protection

Django's template system automatically escapes variables to prevent XSS attacks. Use the `|safe` filter for trusted HTML content:

```html
{{ trusted_html_content | safe }}
```

3. SQL Injection Protection

Django's ORM protects against SQL injection by parameterizing queries. Avoid using raw SQL queries and use Django's query building methods:

```python
# Bad
User.objects.raw('SELECT * FROM auth_user WHERE username = %s' % username)

# Good
User.objects.filter(username=username)
```

4. Clickjacking Protection

Prevent clickjacking attacks by setting the `X-Frame-Options` header to `DENY` or `SAMEORIGIN`:

```python
# settings.py
X_FRAME_OPTIONS = 'DENY'
```

Secure Configuration

1. Secret Key Protection

Keep your Django `SECRET_KEY` secure. Avoid hardcoding it in settings files and use environment variables or a secret management system:

```python
# settings.py
SECRET_KEY = os.environ.get('SECRET_KEY')
```

2. Debug Mode

Disable Django's debug mode (`DEBUG=False`) in production to prevent sensitive information from being exposed:

```python
# settings.py
DEBUG = False
```

Additional Security Measures

1. HTTPS Configuration

Use HTTPS to encrypt communication between the client and server. Configure your web server to use HTTPS and enforce HTTPS redirection:

```python
# settings.py
SECURE_SSL_REDIRECT = True
```

2. Rate Limiting and Captcha

Implement rate limiting and captcha verification for sensitive operations to prevent abuse and brute-force attacks.

3. Security Headers

Set security headers to enhance security:

```python
# settings.py
SECURE_BROWSER_XSS_FILTER = True
SECURE_CONTENT_TYPE_NOSNIFF = True
```

4. Security Auditing and Monitoring

Regularly audit and monitor your application for security vulnerabilities. Use tools like Django Security Middleware and security scanners to identify potential risks.

Securing your Django application is essential to protect it from common security threats and ensure the safety of your users' data. By following best practices such as implementing authentication and authorization, protecting against common security vulnerabilities, configuring secure settings, and implementing additional security measures, you can build a robust and secure Django application. Remember to stay informed about the latest security trends and regularly update your application to address any newly discovered vulnerabilities. With proper security measures in place, you can build trust with your users and safeguard your application against malicious attacks.

Chapter 9

Managing Images, CSS, JavaScript, and Other Static Content

Managing images, CSS, JavaScript, and other static content is essential for creating engaging and interactive web applications in Django full-stack development. Django provides a robust mechanism for serving static files efficiently, allowing you to organize and manage your static content effectively. In this guide, we'll explore how to manage static content in Django, covering the organization of static files, serving static files during development and production, and optimizing the delivery of static content.

Organization of Static Files

Before diving into managing static files in Django, it's essential to organize your static content in a structured manner within your project directory. By convention, Django recommends storing static files in a directory named `static` within each app's directory. Additionally, you can create subdirectories within the `static` directory to further organize your static files based on their purpose or functionality. Here's an example of a typical directory structure for managing static files in a Django project:

```
project/
|-- app1/
|   |-- static/
|   |   |-- app1/
|   |   |   |-- css/
|   |   |   |-- js/
|   |   |   |-- img/
|-- app2/
|   |-- static/
|   |   |-- app2/
|   |   |   |-- css/
|   |   |   |-- js/
|   |   |   |-- img/
|-- static/
|   |-- css/
|   |-- js/
|   |-- img/
```

In this structure:

- Each app (`app1`, `app2`, etc.) has its own `static` directory to store app-specific static files.

- The project-wide `static` directory contains static files that are shared across multiple apps or used globally.

Serving Static Files during Development

During development, Django's built-in development server automatically serves static files from the `STATICFILES_DIRS` and `STATIC_ROOT` directories defined in your project settings. Ensure that you've configured these settings correctly in your `settings.py` file:

```python
# settings.py
import os

STATIC_URL = '/static/'

STATICFILES_DIRS = [
    os.path.join(BASE_DIR, 'static'),
]

STATIC_ROOT = os.path.join(BASE_DIR, 'staticfiles')
```

With this configuration:

- The `STATICFILES_DIRS` setting specifies the directories where Django looks for static files.

- The `STATIC_ROOT` setting specifies the directory where Django collects static files during the `collectstatic` management command.

To serve static files during development, include the following lines in your project's `urls.py` file:

```python
# urls.py
from django.conf import settings
from django.conf.urls.static import static

urlpatterns = [
    # URL patterns for your views
]

if settings.DEBUG:
    urlpatterns += static(settings.STATIC_URL, document_root=settings.STATIC_ROOT)
```

Serving Static Files in Production

In a production environment, it's recommended to serve static files using a dedicated web server or a content delivery network (CDN) for better performance and scalability. Django provides the `collectstatic` management command, which collects static files from all apps and places them into the `STATIC_ROOT` directory. You can then configure your web server to serve static files directly from this directory.

To collect static files, run the following command:

```bash
python manage.py collectstatic
```

This command will copy all static files from the `STATICFILES_DIRS` directories and place them into the `STATIC_ROOT` directory.

Next, configure your web server (e.g., Nginx, Apache) to serve static files directly from the `STATIC_ROOT` directory. Here's an example Nginx configuration:

```
server {
    listen 80;
    server_name example.com;

    location /static/ {
        alias /path/to/staticfiles/;
```

```
    }

    location / {
        # Other configurations for handling dynamic content
    }
```

Replace `/path/to/staticfiles/` with the path to your `STATIC_ROOT` directory.

Optimizing Static Content Delivery

To optimize the delivery of static content and improve performance, consider the following best practices:

1. Use CDN: Use a CDN to cache static files and serve them from edge servers located closer to users, reducing latency and improving load times.

2. Compression: Enable compression (e.g., gzip) for static files to reduce file sizes and minimize bandwidth usage.

3. Cache-Control Headers: Set appropriate `Cache-Control` headers to control caching behavior and specify how long static files should be cached by clients and proxies.

4. Versioning: Use versioning (e.g., file hash, timestamp) for static files to ensure that clients always fetch the latest version of the file, even after updates.

5. Minification: Minify CSS and JavaScript files to remove unnecessary whitespace and reduce file sizes, improving load times.

6. Image Optimization: Optimize images by compressing them and using appropriate image formats (e.g., WebP) to reduce file sizes without compromising quality.

Managing images, CSS, JavaScript, and other static content is crucial for building modern and responsive web applications in Django. By organizing static files in a structured manner, serving static files efficiently during development and production, and optimizing the delivery of static content, you can improve the performance and scalability of your Django applications. Follow the best practices outlined in this guide to effectively manage static content and ensure a seamless user experience for your application's users.

Uploading and Handling User-Generated Content (Media)

Handling user-generated content, such as images, videos, and other media, is a common requirement in web applications. In Django full stack development, managing user-uploaded media involves handling file uploads, storing media files, serving media files, and implementing features like image resizing and file validation. In this guide, we'll explore how to upload and handle user-generated content in a Django application, complete with code examples and best practices.

File Uploads in Django

Django provides a convenient way to handle file uploads using Django forms and models. Let's start by creating a model to represent user-uploaded media:

```python
# models.py
from django.db import models

class Media(models.Model):
    file = models.FileField(upload_to='uploads/')
    uploaded_at = models.DateTimeField(auto_now_add=True)
```

In this model:

- We define a `Media` model with a `FileField` to store the uploaded file.

- The `upload_to` argument specifies the directory where uploaded files will be stored relative to the `MEDIA_ROOT` setting.

Next, let's create a form to handle file uploads:

```python
# forms.py
from django import forms
from .models import Media

class MediaUploadForm(forms.ModelForm):
    class Meta:
        model = Media
        fields = ['file']
```

In this form:

- We create a `MediaUploadForm` class that inherits from `forms.ModelForm`.

- We specify the `Media` model and the `file` field as the form fields.

Handling File Uploads in Views

Now, let's create a view to handle file uploads using the `MediaUploadForm`:

```python
# views.py
from django.shortcuts import render, redirect
from .forms import MediaUploadForm

def upload_media(request):
    if request.method == 'POST':
        form = MediaUploadForm(request.POST, request.FILES)
        if form.is_valid():
            form.save()
            return redirect('upload_success')
    else:
        form = MediaUploadForm()
    return render(request, 'upload_media.html', {'form': form})
```

In this view:

- We handle both GET and POST requests.

- If the form is valid, we save the uploaded file and redirect the user to a success page.

- If the form is not valid or the request is not POST, we render the upload form template with the form.

Serving Media Files

To serve user-uploaded media files in development, you need to configure Django to serve media files from the `MEDIA_ROOT` directory. Add the following settings to your `settings.py` file:

```python
# settings.py
import os

MEDIA_URL = '/media/'
MEDIA_ROOT = os.path.join(BASE_DIR, 'media')
```

Additionally, include the following line in your project's `urls.py` file to serve media files during development:

```python
```

```
# urls.py
from django.conf import settings
from django.conf.urls.static import static

urlpatterns = [
    # URL patterns for your views
]

if settings.DEBUG:
    urlpatterns += static(settings.MEDIA_URL, document_root=settings.MEDIA_ROOT)
```

Uploading and Displaying User-Generated Content

Now, let's create a template to render the file upload form and display uploaded media:

```html
<!-- upload_media.html -->
<!DOCTYPE html>
<html lang="en">
<head>
    <meta charset="UTF-8">
    <meta name="viewport" content="width=device-width, initial-scale=1.0">
    <title>Upload Media</title>
</head>
```

```html
<body>
  <h1>Upload Media</h1>
  <form method="post" enctype="multipart/form-data">
    {% csrf_token %}
    {{ form.as_p }}
    <button type="submit">Upload</button>
  </form>
</body>
</html>
```

Resizing Images

If you're dealing with image uploads, you may want to resize images to reduce file size and ensure consistent dimensions. Django provides the `Pillow` library for image processing. Here's how to resize images using `Pillow`:

```python
# views.py
from PIL import Image

def resize_image(image_path, width, height):
    image = Image.open(image_path)
    image.thumbnail((width, height))
    image.save(image_path)
```

Handling user-generated content, such as media uploads, is a common requirement in web applications. In Django full stack development, you can manage user-uploaded media efficiently using Django's file upload handling mechanisms. By following the steps outlined in this guide, including defining models and forms for handling file uploads, configuring Django settings to serve media files, and implementing features like image resizing, you can effectively manage user-generated content in your Django application. With proper handling of user-generated content, you can enhance the functionality and interactivity of your web application, providing users with a rich and engaging experience.

Optimizing Static Files for Performance

Optimizing static files for performance is crucial for improving the loading speed and overall user experience of your Django web application. In Django full stack development, static files such as CSS, JavaScript, and images play a significant role in shaping the performance of your application. In this guide, we'll explore various techniques and best practices to optimize static files for performance in a Django application, complete with code examples and recommendations.

Minification and Compression

Minification and compression are techniques used to reduce the size of static files, such as CSS and JavaScript, by removing unnecessary whitespace, comments, and other characters without affecting functionality.

Minification

Minification reduces the size of static files by removing unnecessary characters, such as whitespace, comments, and line breaks. You can use tools like `django-compressor` or `django-pipeline` to automatically minify your static files in Django. Here's how to use `django-compressor`:

1. Install `django-compressor`:

```bash
pip install django-compressor
```

2. Add `compressor` to your `INSTALLED_APPS` in `settings.py`:

```python
INSTALLED_APPS = [
    ...
```

```
    'compressor',
    ...
]
```

3. Configure `django-compressor` settings in `settings.py`:

```python
STATICFILES_FINDERS = [
    'compressor.finders.CompressorFinder',
]

COMPRESS_ENABLED = True
COMPRESS_CSS_FILTERS = [
    'compressor.filters.css_default.CssAbsoluteFilter',
    'compressor.filters.cssmin.rCSSMinFilter',
]
COMPRESS_JS_FILTERS = [
    'compressor.filters.jsmin.JSMinFilter',
]
```

Compression

Compression further reduces the size of static files by compressing them using algorithms like Gzip or Brotli. Most modern web servers, such as Nginx or Apache, support compression out of the box. You can enable compression by configuring your web server.

CDN (Content Delivery Network)

Using a Content Delivery Network (CDN) can significantly improve the performance of serving static files by caching them on edge servers located closer to users. Django makes it easy to integrate with CDNs by allowing you to specify the CDN URL for static files.

```python
STATIC_URL = 'https://cdn.example.com/static/'
```

Caching

Caching static files in the client's browser and on intermediary servers can reduce the number of requests and improve load times. You can set appropriate cache-control headers for static files to control caching behavior.

```python
# settings.py
STATICFILES_STORAGE = 'django.contrib.staticfiles.storage.ManifestStaticFilesStorage'
```

```
# Use a versioned URL for static files to leverage browser caching
STATIC_URL = '/static/'

# Set cache-control headers for static files
AWS_HEADERS = {
    'Cache-Control': 'public, max-age=31536000',  # Cache for 1 year
}
```

Image Optimization

Optimizing images can significantly reduce their size without sacrificing quality, leading to faster load times. You can use tools like `Pillow` or online services like TinyPNG to compress and optimize images.

```python
# views.py
from PIL import Image

def optimize_image(image_path):
    image = Image.open(image_path)
    image.save(image_path, optimize=True, quality=85)
```

Lazy Loading

Lazy loading is a technique that defers the loading of non-essential resources, such as images or JavaScript, until they are needed. You can implement lazy loading for images using the `loading="lazy"` attribute in HTML.

```html
<img src="image.jpg" loading="lazy" alt="Lazy-loaded image">
```

Preloading and Prefetching

Preloading and prefetching resources can improve performance by loading critical resources in advance. You can use the `preload` or `prefetch` attributes in HTML to instruct the browser to fetch resources early.

```html
<link rel="preload" href="script.js" as="script">
<link rel="prefetch" href="style.css">
```

Optimizing static files for performance is essential for improving the loading speed and overall user experience of your Django web application. By implementing techniques such as minification, compression, CDN integration, caching, image optimization, lazy loading, preloading, and prefetching, you can significantly reduce load times and enhance the performance of your application. Follow the best practices outlined in this guide to optimize static files effectively and ensure a fast and responsive user experience for your Django application's users.

Chapter 10

Django Admin Panel: Effortless Content Management

Creating a User-Friendly Admin Interface for Content Management

Creating a user-friendly admin interface for content management is essential for efficiently managing data and resources in a Django web application. Django provides a powerful built-in admin interface that allows developers to quickly create an admin panel for managing models and content. In this guide, we'll explore how to customize and enhance the Django admin interface to create a user-friendly experience for content management, complete with code examples and best practices.

Enabling Django Admin

Before customizing the Django admin interface, make sure the admin app is enabled in your Django project's `INSTALLED_APPS` setting:

```python
# settings.py
INSTALLED_APPS = [
    ...
```

```
    'django.contrib.admin',
    ...
]
```

Additionally, ensure that the admin URLs are included in your project's URL configuration:

```python
# urls.py
from django.contrib import admin

urlpatterns = [
    ...
    path('admin/', admin.site.urls),
    ...
]
```

Registering Models with the Admin Interface

To make a model editable in the Django admin interface, register it with the `admin.site.register()` method in the `admin.py` file of your app:

```python
# admin.py
from django.contrib import admin
```

```
from .models import MyModel

admin.site.register(MyModel)
```

Customizing the Admin Interface

Django's admin interface can be customized and extended to meet specific requirements and preferences. Here are some ways to customize the admin interface:

Customizing Model Admin Options

You can customize the appearance and behavior of models in the admin interface by creating a custom `ModelAdmin` class:

```python
# admin.py
from django.contrib import admin
from .models import MyModel

class MyModelAdmin(admin.ModelAdmin):
    list_display = ['name', 'created_at', 'updated_at']
    search_fields = ['name']
    list_filter = ['category']

admin.site.register(MyModel, MyModelAdmin)
```

```

In this example:

- `list_display` specifies the fields to display in the list view of the admin interface.

- `search_fields` adds a search box to filter results based on the specified fields.

- `list_filter` adds filter options to the right sidebar based on the specified fields.

**Customizing Admin Templates**

You can customize the appearance of the admin interface by overriding the default admin templates. Create a directory named `templates/admin` in your project's directory and copy the desired admin templates from the Django source code. You can then modify these templates as needed.

**Adding Inline Editing**

Inline editing allows users to edit related objects directly within the parent object's admin page. You can enable inline editing by using the `InlineModelAdmin` class:
```

```python
# admin.py
from django.contrib import admin
from .models import ParentModel, ChildModel

class ChildModelInline(admin.TabularInline):
    model = ChildModel

class ParentModelAdmin(admin.ModelAdmin):
    inlines = [ChildModelInline]

admin.site.register(ParentModel, ParentModelAdmin)
```

Adding Actions and Filters

You can add custom actions and filters to the admin interface to perform bulk operations and filter results:

```python
# admin.py
from django.contrib import admin
from .models import MyModel

class MyModelAdmin(admin.ModelAdmin):
    list_display = ['name', 'created_at', 'updated_at']
    actions = ['make_published']
```

```
    def make_published(self, request, queryset):
        queryset.update(status='published')
    make_published.short_description = "Mark selected items as published"

admin.site.register(MyModel, MyModelAdmin)
```

Adding Custom Admin Views

You can create custom admin views to perform complex operations or display custom reports:

```python
# admin.py
from django.contrib import admin
from django.http import HttpResponse

class MyModelAdmin(admin.ModelAdmin):
    def custom_report(self, request):
        # Generate custom report
        return HttpResponse("Custom report")

    def get_urls(self):
        urls = super().get_urls()
        custom_urls = [
```

```
        path('custom-report/',
self.admin_site.admin_view(self.custom_report),
name='custom_report'),
    ]
        return custom_urls + urls

admin.site.register(MyModel, MyModelAdmin)
```

Creating a user-friendly admin interface for content management is essential for efficiently managing data and resources in a Django web application. By leveraging Django's built-in admin interface and customizing it to meet specific requirements, you can provide users with a seamless and intuitive experience for managing content. Follow the best practices outlined in this guide to customize and enhance the Django admin interface effectively, ensuring a user-friendly experience for content management in your Django application.

Managing Models and Data Efficiently with the Admin Panel

Managing models and data efficiently with the admin panel is one of the key features of Django full-stack development. The Django admin panel provides a powerful interface for developers and administrators to interact with the application's database models, allowing for easy creation, modification, and deletion of data. In this guide, we'll explore how to efficiently manage models and data using the Django admin panel, complete with code examples and best practices.

Creating and Registering Models

Before managing data with the admin panel, you need to define your database models. Django models represent the structure of your data and are defined in the `models.py` file of your Django app. Here's an example of a simple model definition:

```python
# models.py
from django.db import models

class Product(models.Model):
    name = models.CharField(max_length=100)
    description = models.TextField()
    price = models.DecimalField(max_digits=10, decimal_places=2)
    created_at = models.DateTimeField(auto_now_add=True)
    updated_at = models.DateTimeField(auto_now=True)

    def __str__(self):
        return self.name
```

Next, register the model with the admin panel to make it accessible for data management:

```python
# admin.py
from django.contrib import admin
from .models import Product

admin.site.register(Product)
```

Managing Data in the Admin Panel

Once the model is registered with the admin panel, you can manage data through the admin interface. To access the admin panel, navigate to the `/admin` URL in your browser and log in with a superuser account.

Creating New Objects

To create a new object (record) in the database, click on the "Add" button next to the model name in the admin panel. Fill in the required fields in the form and click the "Save" button to create the object.

Viewing and Editing Objects

To view or edit existing objects, navigate to the list view of the corresponding model in the admin panel. From here, you can view a list of all objects in the database, search for specific objects, and click on an object to view or edit its details.

Deleting Objects

To delete an object, select the checkbox next to the object(s) you want to delete and click the "Delete selected" button at the top or bottom of the list view.

Customizing Model Admin Options

You can customize the behavior and appearance of models in the admin panel by creating a custom `ModelAdmin` class. Here are some common customizations:

Displaying Fields in the List View

```python
# admin.py
from django.contrib import admin
from .models import Product

class ProductAdmin(admin.ModelAdmin):
    list_display = ['name', 'price', 'created_at', 'updated_at']
```

```
admin.site.register(Product, ProductAdmin)
```

Adding Filters and Search

```python
# admin.py
from django.contrib import admin
from .models import Product

class ProductAdmin(admin.ModelAdmin):
    list_display = ['name', 'price', 'created_at', 'updated_at']
    list_filter = ['created_at', 'updated_at']
    search_fields = ['name', 'description']

admin.site.register(Product, ProductAdmin)
```

Customizing the Edit Form

```python
# admin.py
from django.contrib import admin
from .models import Product

class ProductAdmin(admin.ModelAdmin):
    list_display = ['name', 'price', 'created_at', 'updated_at']
```

```
    fields = ['name', 'description', 'price']

admin.site.register(Product, ProductAdmin)
```

Overriding Model Methods

You can override model methods to customize the behavior of objects in the admin panel:

```python
# models.py
from django.db import models

class Product(models.Model):
    name = models.CharField(max_length=100)
    price = models.DecimalField(max_digits=10, decimal_places=2)
    is_discounted = models.BooleanField(default=False)

    def save(self, *args, **kwargs):
        if self.price < 10:
            self.is_discounted = True
        super().save(*args, **kwargs)
```

Managing models and data efficiently with the admin panel is a key aspect of Django full-stack development.

By defining models, registering them with the admin panel, and customizing the admin interface to meet specific requirements, you can streamline the process of data management in your Django application. Follow the best practices outlined in this guide to efficiently manage models and data using the Django admin panel, ensuring a smooth and intuitive experience for administrators and users alike.

Extending the Admin Functionality for Custom Needs

Extending the admin functionality for custom needs is a powerful feature of Django full-stack development. While Django's built-in admin interface provides a robust set of tools for managing models and data, there are often cases where additional customization and functionality are required to meet specific project requirements. In this guide, we'll explore how to extend the admin functionality for custom needs in Django, including customizing admin views, adding custom actions, and integrating third-party packages, complete with code examples and best practices.

Customizing Admin Views

Django allows you to customize admin views by subclassing the `ModelAdmin` class and overriding its methods. This allows you to add custom logic or modify the behavior of admin views. Here's an example of customizing the admin view for a model:

```python
# admin.py
from django.contrib import admin
from .models import Product

class ProductAdmin(admin.ModelAdmin):
    list_display = ['name', 'price', 'created_at', 'updated_at']

    def get_queryset(self, request):
        queryset = super().get_queryset(request)
        # Custom queryset logic
        return queryset.filter(category='electronics')

admin.site.register(Product, ProductAdmin)
```

In this example, we override the `get_queryset()` method to filter the list of products based on a specific category.

Adding Custom Actions

You can add custom actions to the admin interface to perform bulk operations on selected objects. Here's how to define a custom action:

```python
# admin.py
from django.contrib import admin
from .models import Product

def mark_as_discounted(modeladmin, request, queryset):
    queryset.update(is_discounted=True)
mark_as_discounted.short_description = "Mark selected products as discounted"

class ProductAdmin(admin.ModelAdmin):
    list_display = ['name', 'price', 'created_at', 'updated_at']
    actions = [mark_as_discounted]

admin.site.register(Product, ProductAdmin)
```

This adds a custom action named "Mark selected products as discounted" to the admin interface, which marks selected products as discounted when executed.

Adding Custom Admin URLs

You can add custom admin URLs to create additional views and functionality within the admin interface. Here's an example of adding a custom admin URL:

```python
# admin.py
from django.contrib import admin
from django.urls import path
from django.http import HttpResponse

def custom_view(request):
    return HttpResponse("Custom admin view")

class MyAdminSite(admin.AdminSite):
    def get_urls(self):
        urls = super().get_urls()
        custom_urls = [
            path('custom-view/', self.admin_view(custom_view), name='custom_view'),
        ]
        return custom_urls + urls

admin.site = MyAdminSite()

# Register models as usual
admin.site.register(Product)
```

This adds a custom admin URL named "Custom view" that responds with a simple HTTP response when accessed.

Integrating Third-Party Packages

Django's admin interface can be extended further by integrating third-party packages. These packages provide additional features and functionality that may be useful for custom needs. Some popular third-party admin packages include `django-import-export` for importing and exporting data, `django-reversion` for version control of model data, and `django-grappelli` for customizable admin themes.

```bash
pip install django-import-export django-reversion django-grappelli
```

Once installed, follow the documentation of each package to integrate it with your Django project and customize the admin interface as needed.

Extending the admin functionality for custom needs is a powerful feature of Django full-stack development. By customizing admin views, adding custom actions, defining custom admin URLs, and integrating third-party packages, you can tailor the admin interface to meet the specific requirements of your project. Follow the best practices outlined in this guide to extend the admin functionality effectively and efficiently, ensuring a seamless and intuitive experience for administrators and users alike in your Django application.

Chapter 11

Choosing the Right Hosting Platform for Your Django Application

Choosing the right hosting platform for your Django application is crucial for ensuring its performance, scalability, and security. There are several factors to consider when selecting a hosting provider, including server resources, deployment options, pricing, support, and scalability. In this guide, we'll explore how to choose the right hosting platform for your Django application, covering various options and considerations, along with code examples and best practices.

Factors to Consider

Before selecting a hosting platform for your Django application, consider the following factors:

1. Server Resources: Ensure that the hosting provider offers sufficient server resources, including CPU, memory, and disk space, to accommodate your application's requirements.

2. Deployment Options: Look for hosting providers that support easy deployment of Django applications, including options for Git integration, automatic deployment pipelines, and support for popular deployment tools like Docker.

3. Scalability: Choose a hosting platform that allows you to easily scale your application as traffic and resource demands grow. Look for options for horizontal and vertical scaling, auto-scaling, and load balancing.

4. Performance: Evaluate the performance of the hosting platform, including server response times, network latency, and uptime guarantees, to ensure optimal performance for your Django application.

5. Security: Ensure that the hosting provider offers robust security measures, including firewalls, DDoS protection, SSL/TLS encryption, and regular security updates, to protect your application from cyber threats.

6. Support: Look for hosting providers that offer responsive and knowledgeable customer support, including options for live chat, email support, and technical documentation, to assist you with any issues or questions.

7. Cost: Consider the pricing structure of the hosting platform, including upfront costs, monthly fees, usage-based pricing, and any additional charges for add-on services or features, to ensure that it fits within your budget.

Hosting Options

There are several hosting options available for Django applications, each with its own advantages and limitations. Here are some common hosting options to consider:

1. Shared Hosting: Shared hosting plans are cost-effective but may lack the resources and performance needed for high-traffic or resource-intensive Django applications. They are suitable for small-scale projects with low traffic and resource demands.

2. Virtual Private Server (VPS): VPS hosting provides dedicated resources and greater flexibility than shared hosting, allowing you to install custom software and configure server settings. It offers a good balance of performance and cost for medium-scale Django applications.

3. Dedicated Server: Dedicated server hosting provides full control over server resources and configuration, making it suitable for large-scale Django applications with high traffic and resource demands. It offers maximum performance and scalability but may be more expensive than other options.

4. Cloud Hosting: Cloud hosting platforms like AWS, Google Cloud Platform, and Microsoft Azure offer scalable and flexible hosting solutions for Django applications. They provide a wide range of services, including virtual machines, containers, serverless computing, and managed databases, to meet various requirements and use cases.

5. Platform as a Service (PaaS): PaaS providers like Heroku, PythonAnywhere, and DigitalOcean App Platform offer fully managed hosting environments specifically designed for web applications, including Django. They abstract away server management tasks and offer easy deployment options, making them ideal for developers who want to focus on building and deploying their applications without dealing with server configuration.

Example Deployment on Heroku

Let's walk through an example deployment of a Django application on Heroku, a popular PaaS provider:

1. Install the Heroku CLI:

```bash
curl https://cli-assets.heroku.com/install.sh | sh
```

2. Log in to your Heroku account:

```bash
heroku login
```

3. Create a new Heroku app:

```bash
heroku create my-django-app
```

4. Add a `requirements.txt` file containing your Django application's dependencies:

```bash
pip freeze > requirements.txt
```

5. Add a `Procfile` to specify the command to run your Django application:

```
web: gunicorn myproject.wsgi --log-file -
```

```

6. Commit your changes to Git:

```bash
git init
git add .
git commit -m "Initial commit"
```

7. Deploy your Django application to Heroku:

```bash
git push heroku master
```

8. Scale your application to ensure it has sufficient resources:

```bash
heroku ps:scale web=1
```

9. Visit your Django application running on Heroku:

```bash
heroku open
```
```

Choosing the right hosting platform for your Django application is essential for ensuring its performance, scalability, and security. Consider factors such as server resources, deployment options, scalability, performance, security, support, and cost when selecting a hosting provider. Evaluate various hosting options, including shared hosting, VPS, dedicated servers, cloud hosting, and PaaS, to find the best fit for your project's requirements and budget. Follow the best practices outlined in this guide to deploy your Django application successfully and ensure a smooth and reliable hosting experience for your users.

Configuring Your Application for Production Deployment

Configuring your Django application for production deployment is a crucial step to ensure its performance, security, and reliability in a live environment. Production deployment involves optimizing settings, configuring database and static file handling, enabling security features, and setting up logging and monitoring. In this guide, we'll explore how to configure your Django application for production deployment, covering various aspects and best practices, complete with code examples.

Optimizing Settings

Debug Mode

In production, set `DEBUG` to `False` in your `settings.py` to disable detailed error pages and stack traces, improving security and performance.

```python
DEBUG = False
```

Allowed Hosts

Define a list of allowed hosts in `settings.py` to prevent HTTP Host header attacks and specify which host/domain names your application can serve.

```python
ALLOWED_HOSTS = ['example.com', 'www.example.com']
```

Database Configuration

Use a Production Database

In production, use a robust database engine such as PostgreSQL, MySQL, or MariaDB instead of SQLite, which is intended for development purposes.

```python
DATABASES = {
    'default': {
        'ENGINE': 'django.db.backends.postgresql',
        'NAME': 'mydatabase',
        'USER': 'mydatabaseuser',
        'PASSWORD': 'mypassword',
        'HOST': 'localhost',
        'PORT': '5432',
    }
}
```

Static Files Handling

Collectstatic

Run the `collectstatic` management command to gather all static files from your apps into one directory for deployment.

```bash
python manage.py collectstatic
```

Serving Static Files

In production, serve static files using a web server like Nginx or Apache instead of Django's built-in development server.

Security Measures

HTTPS

Enable HTTPS to encrypt communication between clients and your server, preventing data interception and tampering.

CSRF Protection

Ensure CSRF protection is enabled to prevent cross-site request forgery attacks.

```python
CSRF_COOKIE_SECURE = True
```

Session Security

Set `SESSION_COOKIE_SECURE` to `True` to only transmit session cookies over HTTPS.

```python
SESSION_COOKIE_SECURE = True
```

```

### Secure Headers

Use security middleware or third-party packages to set secure HTTP response headers such as HSTS, X-Frame-Options, and X-Content-Type-Options.

### Logging and Monitoring

### Logging Configuration

Configure logging to capture and store application logs, including errors, warnings, and informational messages, for troubleshooting and monitoring.

```python
LOGGING = {
    'version': 1,
    'disable_existing_loggers': False,
    'handlers': {
        'file': {
            'level': 'DEBUG',
            'class': 'logging.FileHandler',
            'filename': '/path/to/django.log',
        },
    },
    'loggers': {
        'django': {

```
            'handlers': ['file'],
            'level': 'DEBUG',
            'propagate': True,
    },
```

Monitoring Tools

Integrate monitoring tools like Sentry or New Relic to track application performance, errors, and exceptions in real-time.

Deployment Automation

Deployment Scripts

Create deployment scripts or use CI/CD tools like Jenkins, Travis CI, or GitHub Actions to automate the deployment process and ensure consistency across environments.

Configuring your Django application for production deployment is essential for ensuring its performance, security, and reliability in a live environment. By optimizing settings, configuring database and static file handling, enabling security features, setting up logging and monitoring, and automating deployment processes, you can deploy your Django application confidently and efficiently. Follow the best practices outlined in this guide to configure your Django application for production deployment successfully and ensure a smooth and reliable experience for your users.

Setting Up Continuous Integration and Continuous Delivery (CI/CD)

Setting up Continuous Integration and Continuous Delivery (CI/CD) for your Django application is crucial for streamlining the development process, ensuring code quality, and automating deployment tasks. CI/CD pipelines automate building, testing, and deploying code changes, leading to faster delivery cycles and improved software reliability. In this guide, we'll explore how to set up CI/CD for your Django application, covering various aspects such as code quality checks, automated testing, and deployment automation, complete with code examples and best practices.

Continuous Integration (CI)

Continuous Integration involves regularly integrating code changes into a shared repository and running automated tests to detect and fix integration errors early in the development process. Here's how to set up CI for your Django application:

1. Version Control

Use a version control system like Git to manage your Django application's source code and collaborate with team members effectively.

```bash
git init
git add .
git commit -m "Initial commit"
```

2. CI Service

Choose a CI service such as GitHub Actions, Travis CI, or CircleCI to automate the CI process. In this example, we'll use GitHub Actions.

3. Configuration

Create a configuration file (e.g., `.github/workflows/ci.yml`) in your repository to define the CI workflow. Here's an example configuration for GitHub Actions:

```yaml
name: CI

on:
```

```yaml
    push:
      branches:
        - main
    pull_request:
      branches:
        - main

jobs:
  build:
    runs-on: ubuntu-latest

    steps:
      - name: Checkout code
        uses: actions/checkout@v2

      - name: Set up Python
        uses: actions/setup-python@v2
        with:
          python-version: 3.x

      - name: Install dependencies
        run: |
          python -m pip install --upgrade pip
          pip install -r requirements.txt

      - name: Run tests
        run: |
          python manage.py test
```

```

This workflow triggers on pushes to the `main` branch and pull requests targeting the `main` branch. It installs dependencies and runs tests using Python 3.

## Continuous Delivery (CD)

Continuous Delivery involves automating the deployment process to release code changes to production quickly and reliably. Here's how to set up CD for your Django application:

### 1. Deployment Environment

Set up a deployment environment for your Django application, such as a cloud hosting platform (e.g., Heroku, AWS, or DigitalOcean) or a dedicated server.

### 2. Deployment Scripts

Create deployment scripts or use deployment tools like Fabric or Ansible to automate deployment tasks such as installing dependencies, migrating the database, collecting static files, and restarting the server.

### 3. CD Service
```

Choose a CD service or deployment tool to automate the deployment process. In this example, we'll use GitHub Actions for CD as well.

4. Configuration

Create a configuration file (e.g., `.github/workflows/cd.yml`) in your repository to define the CD workflow. Here's an example configuration for GitHub Actions:

```yaml
name: CD

on:
  push:
    branches:
      - main

jobs:
  deploy:
    runs-on: ubuntu-latest

    steps:
      - name: Checkout code
        uses: actions/checkout@v2

      - name: Set up Python
```

```yaml
    uses: actions/setup-python@v2
    with:
      python-version: 3.x

  - name: Install dependencies
    run: |
      python -m pip install --upgrade pip
      pip install -r requirements.txt

  - name: Migrate database
    run: python manage.py migrate

  - name: Collect static files
    run: python manage.py collectstatic --noinput

  - name: Restart server
    run: |
      sudo systemctl restart gunicorn
      sudo systemctl restart nginx
```

This workflow triggers on pushes to the `main` branch. It installs dependencies, migrates the database, collects static files, and restarts the server.

Setting up Continuous Integration and Continuous Delivery (CI/CD) for your Django application is essential for automating the development process, ensuring code quality, and automating deployment tasks. By integrating CI tools like GitHub Actions, Travis CI, or CircleCI with your version control system and deployment environment, you can automate building, testing, and deploying code changes, leading to faster delivery cycles and improved software reliability. Follow the best practices outlined in this guide to set up CI/CD for your Django application successfully and streamline your development and deployment workflows.

Chapter 12

Beyond the Basics: Exploring Advanced Django Features

Django REST Framework: Building APIs for Data Exchange

Django REST Framework (DRF) is a powerful toolkit for building Web APIs in Django, providing developers with a flexible and easy-to-use framework for creating RESTful APIs. With DRF, you can quickly and efficiently build APIs for data exchange between different systems, such as web applications, mobile apps, and IoT devices. In this guide, we'll explore how to use Django REST Framework to build APIs for data exchange, covering various aspects such as serialization, views, authentication, and permissions, complete with code examples and best practices.

Installation

First, install Django REST Framework using pip:

```bash
pip install djangorestframework
```

Next, add ``rest_framework`` to the `INSTALLED_APPS` list in your Django project's settings file (`settings.py`).

```python
INSTALLED_APPS = [

    'rest_framework',

]
```

Serialization

Serialization is the process of converting complex data types, such as Django model instances, into JSON, XML, or other formats that can be easily transmitted over the network. DRF provides a powerful serialization mechanism using serializers.

Creating Serializers

```python
from rest_framework import serializers

from .models import Product

class ProductSerializer(serializers.ModelSerializer):

    class Meta:
```

```
        model = Product

        fields = ['id', 'name', 'description', 'price']
```

Views

Views in DRF are similar to Django views but are specifically designed for handling API requests. DRF provides several built-in view classes for handling CRUD operations.

Creating Views

```python
from rest_framework import generics

from .models import Product

from .serializers import ProductSerializer

class ProductListCreateAPIView(generics.ListCreateAPIView):

    queryset = Product.objects.all()

    serializer_class = ProductSerializer

class ProductRetrieveUpdateDestroyAPIView(generics.RetrieveUpdateDestroyAPIView):
```

```
    queryset = Product.objects.all()

    serializer_class = ProductSerializer
```

URLs

Map views to URLs using DRF's built-in routers or Django's URL patterns.

Using DRF Routers

```python
from django.urls import path

from rest_framework.routers import DefaultRouter

from .views import ProductListCreateAPIView, ProductRetrieveUpdateDestroyAPIView

router = DefaultRouter()

router.register(r'products', ProductViewSet)

urlpatterns = [

    path('', include(router.urls)),

]
```

Authentication and Permissions

DRF provides built-in support for authentication and permissions, allowing you to secure your APIs with ease.

Authentication

```python
from rest_framework.authentication import TokenAuthentication
from rest_framework.permissions import IsAuthenticated

class ProductListCreateAPIView(generics.ListCreateAPIView):
    authentication_classes = [TokenAuthentication]
    permission_classes = [IsAuthenticated]
    queryset = Product.objects.all()
    serializer_class = ProductSerializer
```

Permissions

```python
from rest_framework.permissions import IsAdminUser
```

```python
class ProductListCreateAPIView(generics.ListCreateAPIView):
    permission_classes = [IsAdminUser]
    queryset = Product.objects.all()
    serializer_class = ProductSerializer
```

Pagination

DRF provides built-in pagination classes to paginate API responses.

```python
from rest_framework.pagination import PageNumberPagination

class ProductPagination(PageNumberPagination):
    page_size = 10
```

Filtering and Searching

DRF provides filtering and searching capabilities out of the box.

Filtering

```python
from rest_framework.filters import SearchFilter

from django_filters.rest_framework import DjangoFilterBackend

class ProductListCreateAPIView(generics.ListCreateAPIView):
    filter_backends = [DjangoFilterBackend]
    filterset_fields = ['name', 'price']
    queryset = Product.objects.all()
    serializer_class = ProductSerializer
```

Searching

```python
class ProductListCreateAPIView(generics.ListCreateAPIView):
    filter_backends = [SearchFilter]
    search_fields = ['name', 'description']
    queryset = Product.objects.all()
```

```
    serializer_class = ProductSerializer
```

Versioning

DRF supports API versioning to manage changes and updates to your API.

```python
from rest_framework.versioning import URLPathVersioning

class ProductListCreateAPIView(generics.ListCreateAPIView):
    versioning_class = URLPathVersioning
    queryset = Product.objects.all()
    serializer_class = ProductSerializer
```

Throttling

DRF provides built-in throttling classes to limit the number of requests a user can make to your API.

```python
from rest_framework.throttling import UserRateThrottle
```

```
class ProductListCreateAPIView(generics.ListCreateAPIView):
    throttle_classes = [UserRateThrottle]
    queryset = Product.objects.all()
    serializer_class = ProductSerializer
```

Django REST Framework is a powerful toolkit for building APIs for data exchange in Django applications. By leveraging DRF's serialization, views, authentication, permissions, pagination, filtering, searching, versioning, and throttling capabilities, you can create robust and scalable APIs for your web applications, mobile apps, and other systems. Follow the best practices outlined in this guide to use Django REST Framework effectively and efficiently in your Django full stack development projects.

Django Forms: Creating Robust Forms for User Input

Django Forms provide a powerful and flexible way to handle user input in web applications. With Django Forms, you can easily create HTML forms, validate user input, and process form submissions. In this guide, we'll explore how to create robust forms for user input in Django, covering various aspects such as form creation, validation, customization, and integration with views, complete with code examples and best practices.

Form Creation

Django Forms are created by defining Python classes that inherit from `django.forms.Form` or `django.forms.ModelForm`. Each form class represents a specific set of input fields and validation rules.

Creating a Simple Form

```python
# forms.py

from django import forms

class ContactForm(forms.Form):
    name = forms.CharField(label='Your Name', max_length=100)
    email = forms.EmailField(label='Your Email')
    message = forms.CharField(label='Your Message', widget=forms.Textarea)
```

Form Validation

Django Forms provide built-in validation for form fields, ensuring that user input meets specified criteria before processing.

<u>Defining Validation Rules</u>

```python
# forms.py

from django import forms

class ContactForm(forms.Form):
    name = forms.CharField(label='Your Name', max_length=100)
    email = forms.EmailField(label='Your Email')
    message = forms.CharField(label='Your Message', widget=forms.Textarea)

    def clean_message(self):
        message = self.cleaned_data.get('message')
        if 'bad word' in message:
            raise forms.ValidationError("Please refrain from using offensive language.")
        return message
```

Form Rendering

Django Forms can be rendered in HTML templates using template tags and filters provided by the `django.forms` module.

Rendering Forms in Templates

```html
<!-- contact_form.html -->
<form method="post">
    {% csrf_token %}
    {{ form.as_p }}
    <button type="submit">Submit</button>
</form>
```

Form Processing

Django views handle form processing by validating user input, processing form submissions, and rendering appropriate responses.

Handling Form Submissions

```python
```

```python
# views.py
from django.shortcuts import render
from .forms import ContactForm

def contact(request):
    if request.method == 'POST':
        form = ContactForm(request.POST)
        if form.is_valid():
            # Process valid form data
            name = form.cleaned_data['name']
            email = form.cleaned_data['email']
            message = form.cleaned_data['message']
            # Additional processing...
            return render(request, 'success.html')
    else:
        form = ContactForm()
    return render(request, 'contact_form.html', {'form': form})
```
```
```

Customizing Forms

Django Forms can be customized by adding custom validation methods, widgets, and field options.

Customizing Form Fields

```python
# forms.py

from django import forms

class CustomContactForm(ContactForm):

    message = forms.CharField(label='Your Message', widget=forms.Textarea(attrs={'rows': 5}))
```

Formsets

Django Formsets allow you to work with multiple instances of a form on a single page, such as creating or editing multiple objects at once.

Creating a Formset

```python
# forms.py

from django.forms import formset_factory
```

```
from .models import Question

QuestionFormSet = formset_factory(QuestionForm)
```
```

Django Forms provide a robust and flexible way to handle user input in web applications. By creating forms with Django Forms, you can easily define input fields, validate user input, customize form rendering, and process form submissions in Django views. Follow the best practices outlined in this guide to create robust and user-friendly forms for your Django applications, ensuring a smooth and intuitive user experience.

## Django Signals and Middleware: Customizing Django Behavior

Django Signals and Middleware are powerful tools for customizing Django's behavior at various stages of request processing. Signals allow you to execute code in response to certain actions or events, while Middleware allows you to modify request and response objects and perform additional processing before and after view execution. In this guide, we'll explore how to use Django Signals and Middleware to customize Django behavior, covering various aspects such as signal handling, middleware creation, and integration with Django applications, complete with code examples and best practices.

### Django Signals
```

Django Signals provide a way for decoupled applications to send and receive notifications when certain actions or events occur within the Django framework. Signals are useful for implementing cross-application communication and executing code in response to specific events.

Defining Signals

Signals are defined using the `django.dispatch.Signal` class and can be imported from `django.dispatch`.

```python
# signals.py

from django.dispatch import Signal

user_registered = Signal(providing_args=['user'])
```

Connecting Signal Handlers

Signal handlers are functions or methods that are called when a signal is sent. You can connect signal handlers using the `Signal.connect()` method or the `@receiver` decorator.

```python
# handlers.py

from django.dispatch import receiver
```

```python
from .signals import user_registered

@receiver(user_registered)
def send_welcome_email(sender, **kwargs):
    user = kwargs['user']
    # Send welcome email to the newly registered user
```

Sending Signals

To send a signal, use the `Signal.send()` method and provide any necessary arguments.

```python
# views.py
from django.contrib.auth.models import User
from django.shortcuts import render
from .signals import user_registered

def register(request):
    # Process user registration...
    user = User.objects.create(username='example', email='example@example.com')
```

```
        user_registered.send(sender=User, user=user)

        return render(request, 'registration_success.html')
```

Django Middleware

Django Middleware is a framework of hooks into Django's request/response processing. Middleware allows you to modify request and response objects, perform additional processing, and execute code before and after view execution.

Creating Middleware

Middleware is implemented as a Python class that defines one or more methods for processing requests and responses.

```python
# middleware.py

class CustomMiddleware:
    def __init__(self, get_response):
        self.get_response = get_response

    def __call__(self, request):
        # Code to be executed for each request before the view is called
```

```
        response = self.get_response(request)

        # Code to be executed for each response before it is returned to the client

        return response
```

Activating Middleware

Activate middleware by adding it to the `MIDDLEWARE` setting in your Django project's settings file (`settings.py`).

```python
MIDDLEWARE = [

    'myapp.middleware.CustomMiddleware',

]
```

Middleware Example: CORS Headers

As an example, let's create middleware to add CORS (Cross-Origin Resource Sharing) headers to responses, allowing clients from other origins to access resources in your Django application.

```python
```

```python
# middleware.py

class CORSMiddleware:
    def __init__(self, get_response):
        self.get_response = get_response

    def __call__(self, request):
        response = self.get_response(request)
        response['Access-Control-Allow-Origin'] = '*'
        response['Access-Control-Allow-Methods'] = 'GET, POST, OPTIONS'
        response['Access-Control-Allow-Headers'] = 'Content-Type'
        return response
```

Django Signals and Middleware are powerful tools for customizing Django behavior at various stages of request processing. By defining signals and signal handlers, you can execute code in response to specific events within the Django framework. Similarly, by creating middleware classes, you can modify request and response objects, perform additional processing, and execute code before and after view execution. Follow the best practices outlined in this guide to use Django Signals and Middleware effectively in your Django full stack development projects, ensuring a flexible and customizable architecture for your applications.

Chapter 13

Building Your Developer Portfolio: Putting Your Skills to the Test

Choosing a Project Idea and Planning the Development Process

Choosing a project idea and planning the development process are essential steps in any software development endeavor. Whether you're building a personal project, a startup MVP, or a client project, careful planning and consideration of your goals, requirements, and constraints can greatly increase the chances of success. In this guide, we'll explore how to choose a project idea and plan the development process for a Django full stack development project, complete with code examples and best practices.

Choosing a Project Idea

When choosing a project idea, consider the following factors:

1. Interest and Passion: Choose a project idea that aligns with your interests and passions. Building something you're passionate about will keep you motivated throughout the development process.

2. Problem Solving: Identify a problem or pain point that you or others are facing, and build a solution to address it. Solving real-world problems can make your project more meaningful and impactful.

3. Target Audience: Define your target audience and their needs. Consider who will use your application and what features are essential for them.

4. Feasibility: Assess the feasibility of your project idea in terms of technical complexity, resources required, and time constraints. Choose a project idea that you can realistically implement with your skills and resources.

5. Innovation: Look for opportunities to innovate and differentiate your project from existing solutions. Consider adding unique features or taking a different approach to solving a common problem.

Planning the Development Process

Once you've chosen a project idea, it's time to plan the development process. Here are the key steps involved in planning the development process for a Django full stack development project:

1. Define Requirements: Clearly define the requirements and goals of your project. Identify the features and functionality you want to include in your application.

2. Create Wireframes and Mockups: Create wireframes and mockups to visualize the user interface and user experience of your application. Tools like Figma, Sketch, or Adobe XD can be used for this purpose.

3. Database Design: Design the database schema for your application. Identify the models and relationships between them. Use tools like Django's ORM to define your models and database tables.

4. Choose Development Tools: Choose the development tools and technologies you'll use for your project. For a Django full stack development project, you'll need to choose a code editor, version control system (e.g., Git), and deployment platform (e.g., Heroku, AWS).

5. Set Up Project Structure: Set up the project structure for your Django application. Create Django apps for different components of your project (e.g., authentication, API, frontend) and define the URLs, views, templates, and static files for each app.

6. Implement Features: Implement the features and functionality of your application according to the defined requirements. Use Django's built-in features and third-party packages to accelerate development.

7. Testing: Write unit tests, integration tests, and end-to-end tests to ensure the correctness and reliability of your application. Use tools like pytest and Django's testing framework for testing.

8. Deployment: Deploy your Django application to a production environment. Configure settings for security, performance, and scalability. Use continuous integration and continuous deployment (CI/CD) tools for automated testing and deployment.

Example Project Idea: Task Management System

As an example project idea, let's consider building a Task Management System using Django. This application will allow users to create, update, delete, and prioritize tasks, as well as assign tasks to team members and track their progress.

Features:

1. User authentication and authorization
2. CRUD operations for tasks
3. Task prioritization and assignment
4. Team management and collaboration
5. Dashboard with task overview and progress tracking

Choosing a project idea and planning the development process are critical steps in the success of any software development project. By carefully considering your interests, target audience, feasibility, and innovation opportunities, you can choose a project idea that aligns with your goals and objectives. Similarly, by defining requirements, creating wireframes, choosing development tools, setting up project structure, implementing features, testing, and deploying your application, you can plan the development process effectively and ensure a smooth and successful project execution. Follow the best practices outlined in this guide to choose a project idea and plan the development process for your Django full stack development project, and you'll be well on your way to building a successful application.

Implementing Advanced Features and User Experience Enhancements

Implementing advanced features and user experience enhancements is crucial for making your Django application stand out and provide a compelling user experience. From adding real-time updates and notifications to improving accessibility and performance, there are many ways to enhance your Django application. In this guide, we'll explore how to implement advanced features and user experience enhancements in Django full stack development, complete with code examples and best practices.

Real-Time Updates with WebSockets

Adding real-time updates to your Django application allows users to receive instant notifications and updates without refreshing the page. You can achieve this using WebSockets and a WebSocket library like Django Channels.

Setting Up Django Channels

```bash
```

```
pip install channels
```

Example: Real-Time Chat Application

```python
# consumers.py

import json

from channels.generic.websocket import WebsocketConsumer

class ChatConsumer(WebsocketConsumer):
    def connect(self):
        self.accept()

    def disconnect(self, close_code):
        pass

    def receive(self, text_data):
        text_data_json = json.loads(text_data)
        message = text_data_json['message']
        self.send(text_data=json.dumps({
            'message': message
```

        }))
```

## User Authentication and Authorization

Implementing user authentication and authorization ensures that your Django application is secure and only accessible to authorized users.

### Using Django's Built-In Authentication System

```python
# views.py

from django.contrib.auth.decorators import login_required

@login_required
def dashboard(request):
    # Display user-specific dashboard
```

RESTful APIs with Django REST Framework

Building RESTful APIs using Django REST Framework (DRF) allows you to expose your application's data and functionality to other systems or applications.

Creating a RESTful API
```

```python
# serializers.py
from rest_framework import serializers
from .models import Product

class ProductSerializer(serializers.ModelSerializer):
    class Meta:
        model = Product
        fields = ['id', 'name', 'price']

# views.py
from rest_framework import viewsets
from .models import Product
from .serializers import ProductSerializer

class ProductViewSet(viewsets.ModelViewSet):
    queryset = Product.objects.all()
    serializer_class = ProductSerializer
```

Performance Optimization

Improving the performance of your Django application is essential for providing a fast and responsive user experience. You can optimize performance by caching, database optimization, and using efficient algorithms and data structures.

Using Caching

```python
# settings.py

CACHES = {
    'default': {
        'BACKEND': 'django.core.cache.backends.memcached.MemcachedCache',
        'LOCATION': '127.0.0.1:11211',
    }
}
```

Frontend Framework Integration

Integrating frontend frameworks like React or Vue.js with Django allows you to build interactive and dynamic user interfaces.

Using Django as a Backend API

```javascript
// Fetching data from Django API
fetch('/api/products/')
  .then(response => response.json())
  .then(data => console.log(data));
```

Accessibility Improvements

Making your Django application accessible ensures that users with disabilities can use your application effectively. You can improve accessibility by following web content accessibility guidelines (WCAG) and using semantic HTML.

Example: Adding ARIA Attributes

```html
<button aria-label="Search" class="btn">Search</button>
```

Implementing advanced features and user experience enhancements is crucial for making your Django application successful and providing a compelling user experience. By adding real-time updates, implementing user authentication and authorization, building RESTful

APIs, optimizing performance, integrating frontend frameworks, and improving accessibility, you can create a powerful and user-friendly Django application that meets the needs of your users. Follow the best practices outlined in this guide to implement advanced features and user experience enhancements effectively in your Django full stack development projects.

Showcasing Your Skills and Landing Your Dream Job

Showcasing your skills and landing your dream job as a Django full stack developer requires a combination of technical expertise, a strong portfolio, effective communication, and strategic job search tactics. In this guide, we'll explore how to showcase your skills effectively and increase your chances of landing your dream job in Django full stack development, complete with code examples and best practices.

Building a Strong Portfolio

A strong portfolio is essential for showcasing your skills and experience to potential employers. Your portfolio should include:

1. Projects: Showcase your Django projects, including personal projects, open-source contributions, and client work. Highlight the technologies, features, and challenges you've worked on.

2. Code Samples: Include code samples that demonstrate your coding style, best practices, and problem-solving skills. Showcase your understanding of Django, Python, front-end technologies, and database management.

3. Documentation: Provide clear and concise documentation for your projects, including installation instructions, usage guides, and API documentation. This demonstrates your ability to communicate effectively and helps potential employers understand your projects.

Contributing to Open Source

Contributing to open-source projects is an excellent way to showcase your skills, collaborate with other developers, and gain real-world experience. Look for Django-related projects on platforms like GitHub and contribute by fixing bugs, adding features, or improving documentation.

Example: Contributing to Django

```python
# Fixing a bug in Django

# https://github.com/django/django/issues/12345

from django.core.exceptions import ValidationError

def validate_email(value):
    if not value.endswith('@example.com'):
```

```
        raise ValidationError('Email must end with @example.com')
```

Networking and Building Connections

Networking is essential for finding job opportunities and building connections in the Django community. Attend local meetups, conferences, and workshops, join online forums and discussion groups, and participate in community events like DjangoCon.

Example: Joining Django Forums

```plaintext
1. Django Users Google Group: https://groups.google.com/forum/#!forum/django-users
2. Django Subreddit: https://www.reddit.com/r/django/
3. Django IRC Channel: irc://irc.freenode.net/django
```

Creating a Professional Online Presence

Having a professional online presence is crucial for attracting potential employers and showcasing your skills. Create a personal website or blog where you can showcase your projects, share your thoughts on Django development, and demonstrate your expertise.

Example: Personal Website

```html
<!DOCTYPE html>
<html lang="en">
<head>
    <meta charset="UTF-8">
    <meta name="viewport" content="width=device-width, initial-scale=1.0">
    <title>John Doe - Django Developer</title>
</head>
<body>
    <header>
        <h1>John Doe</h1>
        <nav>
            <ul>
                <li><a href="/">Home</a></li>
```

```
        <li><a href="/projects">Projects</a></li>
        <li><a href="/blog">Blog</a></li>
        <li><a href="/contact">Contact</a></li>
      </ul>
    </nav>
  </header>
  <main>
    <h2>About Me</h2>
    <p>I am a Django developer passionate about building web applications with Python.</p>
  </main>
  <footer>
    <p>&copy; 2022 John Doe</p>
  </footer>
</body>
</html>
```

Tailoring Your Resume and Cover Letter

Tailor your resume and cover letter to highlight your relevant skills, experiences, and achievements in Django full stack development. Use action verbs, quantify your accomplishments, and customize your resume and cover letter for each job application.

Example: Resume Bullet Point

- Developed and maintained Django-based web applications, including e-commerce platforms and content management systems, resulting in a 20% increase in user engagement.

Interview Preparation

Prepare for interviews by practicing common interview questions, reviewing Django documentation, and brushing up on your technical skills. Be prepared to discuss your past projects, problem-solving approach, and how you handle challenges in Django development.

Example: Technical Interview Question

Q: How would you optimize the performance of a Django application?

A: I would start by profiling the application to identify bottlenecks and areas for optimization. I would then consider strategies such as caching, database optimization, and using efficient algorithms and data structures. Additionally, I would optimize frontend performance by minimizing HTTP requests, optimizing images and assets, and using lazy loading where appropriate.

Showcasing your skills and landing your dream job in Django full stack development requires a combination of technical expertise, a strong portfolio, effective communication, networking, and interview preparation. By building a strong portfolio, contributing to open-source projects, networking, creating a professional online presence, tailoring your resume and cover letter, and preparing for interviews, you can increase your chances of success in the competitive job market. Follow the best practices outlined in this guide to showcase your skills effectively and stand out as a top candidate in Django full stack development.

Conclusion

In conclusion, diving into the world of Django full stack development with Python is like embarking on a thrilling adventure where creativity meets functionality. Throughout this journey, we've explored the power of Django's robust framework, harnessing its capabilities to build dynamic and scalable web applications with ease.

From laying the foundation with models and databases to crafting intricate views and templates, every step in Django development is a testament to its efficiency and versatility. We've witnessed how Django's ORM simplifies database interactions, allowing developers to focus on building features rather than wrangling with SQL queries.

Moreover, the seamless integration of Django with front-end technologies like HTML, CSS, and JavaScript opens up endless possibilities for creating visually stunning and interactive user interfaces. Whether it's implementing AJAX for smooth asynchronous operations or utilizing Django's built-in template language for dynamic content generation, the synergy between Django and front-end technologies empowers developers to deliver exceptional user experiences.

But Django isn't just about building static websites; it's a framework designed for scalability and extensibility. With Django's modular app structure and support for third-party packages, developers can easily expand the functionality of their applications, whether it's integrating authentication mechanisms, implementing RESTful APIs, or incorporating complex business logic.

Furthermore, Django's emphasis on security ensures that our applications are protected against common vulnerabilities, from cross-site scripting (XSS) to SQL injection attacks. By adhering to Django's best practices and leveraging its built-in security features, we can develop web applications that not only deliver on functionality but also prioritize the safety and privacy of our users' data.

Beyond its technical capabilities, Django embodies the spirit of collaboration and community-driven innovation. With a vast ecosystem of libraries, documentation, and online resources, developers have access to a wealth of knowledge and support to overcome challenges and push the boundaries of what's possible.

As we reach the culmination of our Django journey, it's important to reflect on the lessons learned and the skills acquired. Through perseverance and experimentation, we've honed our abilities as full stack developers, gaining a deeper understanding of web development principles and best practices.

But the journey doesn't end here; it's merely the beginning of a lifelong pursuit of mastery and innovation. With Django as our trusty companion, we're equipped to tackle the challenges of tomorrow's web development landscape, armed with the knowledge and expertise to bring our ideas to life in the digital realm.

In the ever-evolving world of technology, one thing remains constant: the transformative power of Django and Python in shaping the future of web development. So let's continue to push the boundaries, challenge the status quo, and embark on new adventures in the world of Django full stack development. The possibilities are limitless, and the journey ahead is bound to be nothing short of extraordinary.

Appendix

Common Python Libraries and Tools for Web Development

Python, with its simplicity and versatility, has become a powerhouse for web development. When combined with frameworks like Django, it offers a robust ecosystem of libraries and tools that streamline the development process. Let's explore some of the most common Python libraries and tools used in Django full stack development.

Django

Django is a high-level Python web framework that encourages rapid development and clean, pragmatic design. It follows the "batteries-included" philosophy, providing developers with everything they need to build web applications quickly and efficiently. Here's a brief overview of Django's core components:

Models

```python
from django.db import models

class Product(models.Model):
    name = models.CharField(max_length=100)
```

price = models.DecimalField(max_digits=10, decimal_places=2)
```

### Views

```python
from django.shortcuts import render
from .models import Product
def product_list(request):
    products = Product.objects.all()
    return render(request, 'product_list.html', {'products': products})
```

Templates

```html
<!-- product_list.html -->
{% for product in products %}
    {{ product.name }} - ${{ product.price }}
{% endfor %}

```

URLs

```python

from django.urls import path

from .views import product_list

urlpatterns = [

  path('products/', product_list, name='product_list'),

]
```

Admin Interface

```python

from django.contrib import admin

from .models import Product

admin.site.register(Product)
```

Django REST Framework

Django REST Framework is a powerful toolkit for building Web APIs in Django. It provides serializers for
```

handling complex data structures and authentication mechanisms for securing APIs. Here's a simple example of using Django REST Framework:

```python
from rest_framework import serializers, viewsets

from .models import Product

class ProductSerializer(serializers.ModelSerializer):
    class Meta:
        model = Product
        fields = ['Id', 'name', 'price']

class ProductViewSet(viewsets.ModelViewSet):
    queryset = Product.objects.all()
    serializer_class = ProductSerializer
```

Celery

Celery is a distributed task queue that is commonly used for handling asynchronous tasks in web applications. It can be integrated with Django to perform background processing, such as sending emails or processing large datasets, without blocking the main application. Here's how you can use Celery in Django:

```python
# tasks.py
from celery import shared_task

@shared_task
def send_email(subject, message, recipient):
    # Send email implementation
    pass
```

```python
# views.py
from .tasks import send_email

def send_email_view(request):
    send_email.delay('Subject', 'Message', 'recipient@example.com')
    return HttpResponse('Email sent successfully!')
```

Django Debug Toolbar

Django Debug Toolbar is a configurable set of panels that display various debug information about the current request/response cycle. It can be extremely helpful for debugging and optimizing Django applications during development. Here's how you can integrate Django Debug Toolbar into your Django project:

```python
# settings.py

if DEBUG:
    INSTALLED_APPS += ['debug_toolbar']

    MIDDLEWARE += ['debug_toolbar.middleware.DebugToolbarMiddleware']

    INTERNAL_IPS = ['127.0.0.1']
```

Django Filter

Django Filter provides a simple way to filter down queryset based on user input. It's particularly useful when dealing with large datasets or building search functionality in Django applications. Here's a simple example of using Django Filter:

```python
import django_filters
```

```
from .models import Product

class ProductFilter(django_filters.FilterSet):
    class Meta:
        model = Product
        fields = ['name', 'price']
```

Django CORS Headers

Django CORS Headers is a Django application for handling Cross-Origin Resource Sharing (CORS), which is necessary when your frontend code, running in a browser, makes requests to a different origin than the one serving the frontend. Here's how you can use Django CORS Headers:

```python
# settings.py

CORS_ORIGIN_ALLOW_ALL = True
```

Django Allauth

Django Allauth is an authentication system for Django that provides support for social authentication, like logging in with Google or Facebook, as well as email authentication. It's highly customizable and integrates seamlessly with Django projects. Here's how you can use Django Allauth:

```python
# settings.py

INSTALLED_APPS += ['allauth', 'allauth.account', 'allauth.socialaccount']

AUTHENTICATION_BACKENDS = [

    'django.contrib.auth.backends.ModelBackend',

'allauth.account.auth_backends.AuthenticationBackend

]
```

Python offers a plethora of libraries and tools for web development, and when combined with Django, the possibilities are endless. Whether you're building a simple blog or a complex web application, these libraries and tools can help you streamline the development process, improve code quality, and deliver exceptional user experiences. By leveraging the power of Python and Django, you can bring your web development projects to life with ease and efficiency.

Troubleshooting Tips and Error Handling in Django

Error handling and troubleshooting are essential skills for any Django developer. In the process of building web applications, you're bound to encounter errors and unexpected behavior. Knowing how to diagnose and resolve issues efficiently can save you time and frustration. In this guide, we'll explore some common troubleshooting tips and best practices for error handling in Django.

1. Debugging

Django provides a built-in debug mode that displays detailed error pages with stack traces, request information, and settings. To enable debug mode, set `DEBUG = True` in your settings file. While debug mode is invaluable during development, remember to disable it in production for security reasons.

```python
# settings.py

DEBUG = True
```

2. Logging

Logging is a crucial tool for tracking down errors and debugging issues in Django applications. Django uses the Python standard logging library, allowing you to configure logging levels, handlers, and formatters to suit your needs. Here's an example of configuring logging in Django:

```python
# settings.py

import logging

LOGGING = {
    'version': 1,
    'disable_existing_loggers': False,
    'handlers': {
        'file': {
            'level': 'DEBUG',
            'class': 'logging.FileHandler',
            'filename': '/path/to/django.log',
        },
    'loggers': {
        'django': {
            'handlers': ['file'],
```

```
            'level': 'DEBUG',

            'propagate': True,

    },
```

3. Error Pages

Customizing error pages improves the user experience and provides helpful information when something goes wrong. Django allows you to define custom error views for different HTTP error codes. Here's an example of customizing the 404 page:

```python
# views.py

from django.shortcuts import render

def error_404_view(request, exception):
    return render(request, '404.html', status=404)
```

```html
<!-- 404.html -->
<!DOCTYPE html>
```

```
<html>
<head>
    <title>Page Not Found</title>
</head>
<body>
    <h1>404 - Page Not Found</h1>
    <p>The page you are looking for does not exist.</p>
</body>
</html>
```

4. Django Debug Toolbar

Django Debug Toolbar is a handy tool for inspecting the performance and behavior of Django applications. It provides detailed information about database queries, HTTP requests, template rendering, and more. To install Django Debug Toolbar, use:

```bash
pip install django-debug-toolbar
```

Then, configure it in your `settings.py`:

```python
# settings.py
if DEBUG:
    INSTALLED_APPS += ['debug_toolbar']
    MIDDLEWARE += ['debug_toolbar.middleware.DebugToolbarMiddleware']
    INTERNAL_IPS = ['127.0.0.1']
```

5. Database Errors

Database errors are common in Django applications, especially during migrations or complex queries. When encountering database-related issues, it's essential to check the database configuration, connection settings, and SQL queries. Use Django's built-in `manage.py` commands to inspect and troubleshoot database operations:

```bash
python manage.py makemigrations

python manage.py migrate

python manage.py sqlmigrate <app_name> <migration_number>
```

```
python manage.py shell
```

6. Django Management Commands

Django management commands are powerful tools for performing administrative tasks and troubleshooting issues. You can create custom management commands to automate repetitive tasks or diagnose specific problems. Here's an example of creating a custom management command to analyze database performance:

```python
# myapp/management/commands/analyze_database.py

from django.core.management.base import BaseCommand
from django.db import connection

class Command(BaseCommand):
    help = 'Analyzes database performance'

    def handle(self, *args, **options):
        with connection.cursor() as cursor:
            cursor.execute("ANALYZE;")
        self.stdout.write(self.style.SUCCESS('Database analyzed successfully'))
```

```

Run the custom management command using:

```bash

python manage.py analyze_database

```

7. Third-party Packages

When using third-party packages in your Django project, ensure they are compatible with your Django version and dependencies. Read the documentation carefully, check for any reported issues or bugs, and test thoroughly before deploying to production. If you encounter errors related to third-party packages, consult the package's documentation, GitHub repository, or community forums for guidance.

8. Stack Overflow and Community Forums

Stack Overflow and Django community forums are valuable resources for troubleshooting specific issues and seeking help from experienced developers. Before posting a question, search for similar topics to see if your problem has already been addressed. Provide clear and concise details, including error messages, code snippets, and steps to reproduce the issue, to receive accurate and timely assistance from the community.
```

Troubleshooting and error handling are integral parts of Django development. By following these tips and best practices, you can effectively diagnose and resolve issues in your Django applications, ensuring smooth operation and a seamless user experience. Remember to leverage built-in debugging tools, customize error pages, utilize logging for tracking errors, and seek assistance from the Django community when needed. With a proactive approach to troubleshooting, you'll be well-equipped to tackle any challenges that arise during Django development.

Glossary of terms

Glossary of Terms in Django Full Stack Development with Python

Django:

Django is a high-level Python web framework that enables rapid development of secure and maintainable web applications. It follows the model-view-template (MVT) architectural pattern and includes various built-in features for database management, URL routing, form handling, and authentication.

Model:

In Django, a model is a Python class that represents a database table. It defines the structure and behavior of the data stored in the database, including fields, relationships, and constraints. Django's Object-Relational Mapping (ORM) simplifies database interactions by abstracting away the need to write SQL queries manually.

View:

A view in Django is a Python function or class-based view that receives HTTP requests and returns HTTP responses. Views encapsulate the logic for processing user input, interacting with models, and rendering templates. They serve as the bridge between the presentation layer (templates) and the data layer (models) in the MVT architecture.

Template:

Templates in Django are HTML files with embedded Django template language syntax. They define the presentation layer of a web application, including the layout, structure, and dynamic content. Django's template engine allows for the insertion of variables, control structures, and filters to generate dynamic HTML content based on data passed from views.

URL Dispatcher:

The URL dispatcher in Django is responsible for mapping URLs to views within a web application. It defines a set of URL patterns using regular expressions or simple strings and routes incoming HTTP requests to the appropriate view functions or class-based views. URL dispatching is configured in the project's URL configuration file (`urls.py`).

QuerySet:

A QuerySet in Django is a representation of a database query that retrieves a set of objects from a database table. It allows for filtering, sorting, and manipulating data using a fluent API similar to SQL. QuerySets are lazy-evaluated, meaning that database queries are executed only when necessary, optimizing performance.

Migration:

Migrations in Django are files generated by the `makemigrations` command that describe changes to the database schema. They allow for seamless management of database schema updates, including creating, modifying, and deleting database tables and fields. Migrations ensure data consistency and facilitate collaborative development across multiple environments.

Form:

Forms in Django are Python classes that encapsulate HTML form logic and validation rules. They provide a convenient way to handle user input, validate data, and interact with models. Django's form handling framework includes built-in form classes, field types, and validation mechanisms for creating and processing web forms efficiently.

Authentication:

Authentication in Django refers to the process of verifying the identity of users accessing a web application. Django provides a robust authentication system with built-in support for username/password authentication, session management, and user permissions. Additionally, Django offers third-party authentication backends for integrating with external authentication providers like OAuth and LDAP.

Middleware:

Middleware in Django is a framework of hooks that intercept HTTP requests and responses passing through a web application. Middleware can perform preprocessing tasks, modify request or response objects, or implement cross-cutting concerns such as authentication, caching, and security. Django's middleware architecture allows for extensibility and customization of request/response handling.

Admin Interface:

The Django admin interface is a built-in feature that provides a graphical user interface for managing Django models and data. It offers an out-of-the-box administration panel with CRUD (Create, Read, Update, Delete) functionality for database records, customizable list views, filters, and search capabilities. The admin interface is automatically generated based on registered models and can be customized using ModelAdmin classes.

Serializer:

Serializers in Django are components responsible for converting complex data types (such as Django model instances) into native Python data types (such as dictionaries) that can be easily rendered into JSON or other formats. Serializers facilitate the process of data serialization and deserialization in Django REST Framework views and APIs, ensuring seamless data exchange between the server and client.

Template Tag:

Template tags in Django are special syntax elements used within Django templates to perform logic, iterate over data, or include other templates. Template tags are enclosed within `{% %}` for control flow statements and `{{ }}` for variable interpolation. Django provides a wide range of built-in template tags for common tasks, such as looping, conditional rendering, and URL resolution.

Context Processor:

A context processor in Django is a Python function that adds data to the context of every template rendered within a Django application. Context processors run before rendering each template and can inject dynamic data or settings into the template context. Context processors are defined in Python modules and registered in the `context_processors` setting in `settings.py`.

URL Namespace:

A URL namespace in Django is a way to organize and group URLs within a web application to prevent naming conflicts and improve readability. By defining namespaces for sets of related URLs, developers can create modular and maintainable URL configurations. URL namespaces are configured using the `namespace` parameter in the `include()` function within URL patterns.

Static Files:

Static files in Django are assets such as CSS stylesheets, JavaScript scripts, images, and other resources used by a web application. Django provides a built-in mechanism for serving static files during development and production. Static files are typically stored in the `static` directory within Django apps and served using the `staticfiles` app and `static` template tag.

Middleware:

Middleware is a framework of hooks into Django's request/response processing. It's a light, low-level plugin system for globally altering Django's input or output.

Context:

A dictionary-like object that contains all template variables and their respective values, which are accessible within a template. Context is passed from views to templates to dynamically generate HTML content.

Signals:

Signals are used for allowing decoupled applications to get notified when certain actions occur elsewhere in the application. Django provides a set of built-in signals that can be used to trigger custom actions in response to model events, such as saving, deleting, or updating objects.

Reverse URL Resolution:

Reverse URL resolution is the process of generating a URL based on a view name and optional parameters. It allows developers to reference views by their names rather than hard-coding URLs in templates or views, improving maintainability and flexibility. Django's reverse URL resolution is performed using the `reverse()` function or the `{% url %}` template tag.

CSRF Protection:

Cross-Site Request Forgery (CSRF) protection is a security measure in Django that prevents unauthorized submission of forms by attackers. Django automatically adds CSRF tokens to HTML forms, which are validated on form submission to ensure that the request originated from the same site. CSRF protection is enabled by default in Django and can be customized or disabled if necessary.

Middleware:

Middleware is a framework of hooks into Django's request/response processing. It's a light, low-level plugin system for globally altering Django's input or output.

Context:

A dictionary-like object that contains all template variables and their respective values, which are accessible within a template. Context is passed from views to templates to dynamically generate HTML content.

Signals:

Signals are used for allowing decoupled applications to get notified when certain actions occur elsewhere in the application. Django provides a set of built-in signals that can be used to trigger custom actions in response to model events, such as saving, deleting, or updating objects.

Reverse URL Resolution:

Reverse URL resolution is the process of generating a URL based on a view name and optional parameters. It allows developers to reference views by their names rather than hard-coding URLs in templates or views, improving maintainability

www.ingramcontent.com/pod-product-compliance
Lightning Source LLC
Chambersburg PA
CBHW031608210526
45464CB00004B/1484